Katharina Pilhofer

Cultural Knowledge – A Critical Perspective on the Concept as a Foundation for Respect for Cultural Differences

Diplomica® Verlag GmbH

Pilhofer, Katharina: Cultural Knowledge - A Critical Perspective on the Concept as a Foundation for Respect for Cultural Differences, Hamburg, Diplomica Verlag GmbH 2011

ISBN: 978-3-8428-6263-0
Druck: Diplomica® Verlag GmbH, Hamburg, 2011

Bibliografische Information der Deutschen Nationalbibliothek:
Die Deutsche Nationalbibliothek verzeichnet diese Publikation in der Deutschen Nationalbibliografie; detaillierte bibliografische Daten sind im Internet über http://dnb.d-nb.de abrufbar.

Die digitale Ausgabe (eBook-Ausgabe) dieses Titels trägt die ISBN 978-3-8428-1263-5 und kann über den Handel oder den Verlag bezogen werden.

TABLE OF CONTENTS

Abbreviations

ICT   Intercultural Training

IM   International Management

PCT   Post-Colonial Theory

RQ   Research Question

1 Introduction

1.1 BACKGROUND AND PROBLEM STATEMENT

Recent global economic developments have led to a shift in focus from the local to the global level and international companies are sending more and more of their employees abroad to take on international assignments ((Caligiuri 2000), (Dumont, Lemaître 2005), (Shaffer et al. 2006)). Simultaneously, the interest in inter- and cross-cultural topics has increased in response to the significant changes that have occurred in the context of business operations. One consequence of these changes entails that employees are increasingly exposed to situations where they deal with people of various cultural backgrounds.

Scholars in the field of cross-cultural research have investigated the processes underlying intercultural encounters. They strive to come up with strategies that help dealing with such situations. Authors state that intercultural communication may lead to misunderstandings and miscommunication when people of different cultural backgrounds interact (for example (Black, Mendenhall 1990), (Gudykunst, Mody 2002), (Soderberg, Holden 2002)). Miscommunication arises if one is unaware of cultural differences and therefore perceives the counterpart's perspective to be similar to her/his own. Culture may function as a "filter" when the sender encodes and the receiver decodes a message. Meaning is distorted and interpreted in a wrong way if the filter is not understood (Loosemore, Lee 2002).

The common solution suggested by cross-cultural researchers is the accumulation of knowledge on cultural differences. The latter is seen to have an impact on intercultural communication. The knowledge in turn is assumed to make the situation transparent and "manageable" (for example (Gudykunst 1995), (Leiba-O'Sullivan 1999), (Morris, Robie 2001)). Consequently, the supply of knowledge about cultural differences has grown extensively. Thereby represent cross-national comparisons the most influencing stream that focus on the variation of values across national cultures (Sackmann, Phillips 2004).[1] The most widely known research on the subject is that of Geert Hofstede where he introduced the concept of "cultural dimensions" (see (Hofstede 1980), (Hofstede 1991)). In Hofstede's study, five different cultural dimensions that affect the communicative behaviour of individuals were identified. The popularity of his approach is impressive mainly because it

---

[1] Other streams focus on binational (two particular cultures) settings or engage a multiple culture perspective (including professional culture for example). For an overview see Sackmann and Philips, S. 2004.

is easily replicated, extended, and confirmed (Soendergaard 1994). Hofstede's research represents the most cited and popular theory when it comes to intercultural differences (Morris, Robie 2001). However there are two more important scholars in the field: Edward T. Hall and Fons Trompenaars. All three scholars developed cultural dimensions that are supposed to influence the individual in (intercultural) communication. Their research has been identified with the paradigm of "structural functionalism" (Westwood, Jack 2007). Structural functionalism emphasizes "the view that culture, including the social order, composes a coherent, inclusive system" (Encyclopaedia Britannica 2010). Following this definition, a culture is understood as a closed system that shares norms, values and customs with all members of that cultural group. This means that it is possible to observe differences among different cultures.

The acquisition of knowledge as introduced by Hofstede, Hall and Trompenaars mainly takes place in Intercultural Training (ICT). The "founder" and father of the ICT concept, Edward T. Hall, explains its goal:

> "Preparing people for service overseas is to open their eyes and sensitize them to the subtle qualities of behaviour [...] that so often build up feelings of frustration and hostility in other people with a different culture. [...] We need a frame of reference that will enable us to observe and learn the significance of differences in manners" ((Hall 1955), p. 89).

Hall states that ICT aims to prepare people for intercultural settings in order to prevent emotional discomfort. However ICT also serves as a foundation for future success in intercultural environments in order to be competitive in the international market ((Black, Mendenhall 1990), (Morris, Robie 2001), (Tung 1987)). Cultural knowledge presents the main content taught in ICT.

Cultural knowledge as it is taught in ICT constitutes the main interest of this book. The expression is therefore used many times. This term is operationally defined in the study as scientific knowledge on cultural dimensions that has an impact on intercultural communication. In this context, it therefore does not pertain to anthropological aspects or "do's and don'ts" in a foreign culture. It merely represents a comprehension of the most important factors influencing intercultural communication in the business world. (for a detailed explanation see 4.1 and 4.2).

This book will take a closer look at cultural knowledge as it is used in ICT and critically reflect on the foundations of its conceptualization. I will investigate cultural knowledge in terms of its contribution to the development of intercultural relations based on respect for cultural differences. The use of the word "respect" in this context connotes tolerance for cultural differences. Respect for cultural differences occurs if one is willing to ascribe equal rights to other culturally influenced ways of doing things. Differences are recognized and their freedom is granted.

The idea for this book was inspired by a lecture on "Diversity Management" at Copenhagen Business School. During this lecture, the students were introduced to the philosophy of Emmanuel Levinas. The lecture made me, the author of this book, immediately experience an enormous respect and appreciation for his theory. Levinas claims that everybody is radically different and any attempt to comprehend differences will result in a closed system (totality). He argues that ontology cannot account for the otherness of the other person. His main interest concerns the ethical relationship between individuals where otherness is given room. In that way one is able to responsively interact with other individuals without trying to comprehend differences.

Due to the appreciation of Levinas' theory I started to reflect on cultural knowledge. During my time as a student I was introduced to cultural knowledge researched by Hofstede, Hall and Trompenaars. So far I had always assumed that this knowledge on cultural differences would be enough to develop relations based on respect for cultural differences. However, Levinas introduced me to a different perspective. I started to wonder whether the knowledge I had acquired would actually facilitate – as I had always assumed and was taught by my professors – or rather hinder a relation to members of foreign cultures in a responsible way. Because of this I decided to take a closer look at cultural knowledge as a subject introduced in the university as well as it is taught in ICT. The interest and approach of this book are hereby outlined in the following section.

1.2   INTEREST AND APPROACH OF THE BOOK

This section of the chapter outlines the main focus of interest of this book and the approach used in dealing with the subject matter.

As earlier stated, the author's fascination with Levinas' philosophy was inspired by a lecture on Levinasian ethics. He advocates interpersonal interactions based on respect and openness for differences. Further he denies any ontological approach to difference since it cannot account for the otherness of the counterpart. Ontology is therefore questionable when it comes to the treatment of others in a respectful way. Since cultural knowledge represents an ontological approach I started to wonder how these theories promote interactions based on respect for cultural differences. All the while, I had assumed that cultural knowledge represents the most important foundation for respect since it creates consciousness of cultural differences. In this manner it creates an imaginative room where a person can respect another person regardless of cultural differences.

Cultural knowledge has extensively been lectured at university and in ICT while the latter is mainly conducted in business environments. This shows an enormous trust in the potential of the discourse to support individuals in intercultural encounters. I intend to investigate cultural knowledge with the end view of finding out how cultural knowledge is representative of cultures and whether this is put to use in a respectful way. Acquiring knowledge of cultural differences is commonly equalized with respect for the same (Day 1998). Hence, the acquisition of cultural knowledge should serve as a significant foundation for intercultural encounters based on respect. Reliance on cultural knowledge can provide insight into cultural differences that one can apply in order to respectfully interact with people from other cultures. The term "respect" in this book does therefore not only account for intercultural interactions but also for the representation of cultures. Respect in this manner is understood as a description of cultural dimensions that give an accurate and true reflection of reality. In so doing, people pay respect to cultural difference by giving room to the same. Respect in interactions is achievable if the individual who has adopted cultural knowledge is given the means to respectfully interact with members of foreign cultures. This means that the individual tolerates the difference without any intention to change or manipulate and acknowledges the existence of the difference as an equal right. A respectful representation therefore becomes an important basis for respecting cultural differences.

In effect, this book aims to investigate the limitations of cultural knowledge and points out the consequences for its practical transition in intercultural encounters. It will be argued that scholars consider cultural knowledge as a threat. The study will further reveal how cultural dimensions are accompanied by subliminal interpretations and are homogenized as well as simplified in what they represent. This might seem harsh to the reader but it is important to note that despite the critical approach adopted by the study, there is no intention to generally question the idea to deliver some kind of support for intercultural encounters. Support is considered as a very important and helpful factor since cultural differences can be very confusing and intimidating for the individual in a foreign country or intercultural setting. The intention of this book is to disrupt the ongoing unquestioned dominance of cultural knowledge by pointing out limitations that accompany this concept. Further, the implications for the idea of intercultural encounters based on respect will be discussed. The main argument here is that the limitations are rooted in the West's predominant interest on control. This prevents a respectful representation of cultures since the goal of control is ascribed high(er) importance. Respect is facilitated as long as it does not compromise interests of control. This ultimately leads to consequences that rather prevent than support interactions based on respect.[2]

It is my conviction that a critical stance on cultural knowledge will provide impulses for the liberation of the discourse and open ways that advance respectfulness in intercultural encounters. If ICT and university courses on intercultural management continue to use and lecture about cultural knowledge as extensively as they have done in the past, it is time for such a critical reflection.

At the end of this book, the reader shall understand the extent to which cultural knowledge represents cultures in a respectful way and whether this helps or prevents the development of intercultural encounters based on respect for cultural difference. To attain such, the book invokes Post-colonial Theory (PCT) and its main argumentation. PCT will be of help in this book to address and reflect on cultural knowledge. PCT describes how a Western perspective has framed cultural identities and how these representations are flawed by colonial thinking. It concerns itself with the "effects of colonization on cultures and societies" ((Ashcroft, Griffiths & Tiffin 1998), p.186). The term signifies the political, linguistic and cultural experience of former colonized societies. However it is not only the description of these processes, but also, as Westwood et al. remarked, the

> "[deployment of] diverse theoretical and political resources to interrogate, intervene in and transform the continued power asymmetries, imbalances and repressions, and effects of contemporary neo-colonialism, and other forms of imperialism" ((Westwood, Jack 2007), p. 247).

Since cultural knowledge has mainly been developed by Western scholars, it is also the interest of the book to investigate how their (cultural) background influenced cultural knowledge and the extent to which interests on power and control are an issue. PCT

---

[2] I will state the term "the West" many times in this book and in that regard refer to the "Western world", meaning North America and most of the European countries.

represent a valuable theoretical background for this book, because it critically reflects on Western rationality. In particular, it discusses how the West was engaged with former colonized countries and today with the rest of the world. Since cultural knowledge represents a Western "engagement" with (all) cultures in the world there is an interesting connection between the two. The study will point out observations regarding the extent to which cultural knowledge mirrors some of the PCT-arguments. Afterwards the author is going to discuss the consequences for intercultural interactions based on respect. These consequences particularly affect the students of cultural knowledge.

The study further invokes Emmanuel Levinas' philosophy of ethics. Levinasian ethics represent merely an approach towards an ethical experience of the Other.[3] While PCT mainly focuses on revealing aspects of power and control, Levinasian ethics approaches an ethical relation to difference. It therefore also represents a suggestion or solution in that regard. However Levinas' work is rooted in a critical stance towards knowledge creation about the Other and this is where PCT and Levinas agree. His philosophy of ethics represents a meta-theory of PCT since both share a fundamental criticism of how cultures are rendered and represented in a limited and one-sided way in today's Western world. Levinas however questioned the idea of representing cultures and gathering knowledge in general (Critchley, Bernasconi 2002). He believes that the Other is transcendent to us. There is always something we cannot comprehend with our understanding and frame in categories. He declared that comprehension in that regard is beyond our understanding. If one tries to comprehend the Other, it will happen in one's own categories. The Other would turn into a different version of the same and incomprehensible aspects could not be accounted for. Instead, Levinas advises each individual to act "re-sponsibly" towards the Other by being open to "otherness".[4] This means that everyone is able to give attention to an ethical relationship to difference. Thus, any attempt to understand the Other would be harmful and cannot account for an ethical experience of the Other.

Levinas' approach is rooted in a critique of the scientific representations of the Other. In this sense, Levinasian ethics can further inform the discussion on cultural knowledge and supplement the analysis done from a PCT perspective. Levinasian ethics can contribute to an understanding where intercultural relations are interactions between human beings that

---

[3] The "Other" is written with a capital letter in order to point at the Levinasian understanding of the term. An explanation what this means will follow.

[4] The word "re-sponsibly" is cut in order to emphasize Levinas' idea to respond (to answer, react) to the Other in a responsive way.

deserve first and foremost attention to respect and humanity instead of control and management. In that regard, Levinasian ethics could be understood as a "best practice example" when it comes to interactions based on respect. However, the philosophy of Levinas is very complex and challenging to put into practice. And it is not the intention of this book to suggest how one is supposed to interact ethically with others considering their cultural differences. Nonetheless, it employs his theory in so far as it is a reminder to all regarding the importance of ethics in (intercultural) human interactions. The analysis of cultural knowledge will mainly refer to the critique of Levinas on knowledge gathering in terms of (cultural) representations. However, a thorough understanding of his philosophy is necessary in order to follow his critique. The philosophy of Levinas is introduced in the literature review. The author will also integrate the main points of his approach in the analysis of cultural knowledge.

The analyzed data in this book mainly consists of cultural knowledge itself. The book will analyze the main research in the field and cite authors who have discussed the purpose of cultural knowledge. Further qualitative data was obtained from questionnaires and interviews with people who are extensively exposed to intercultural settings in their daily work and/or have learned about cultural knowledge in ICT or at the university. The interviews will serve to illustrate the arguments made. Hence they are *not* supposed to lead to any new insights. Rather they are applied to serve as illustrations and "prove" the points made since they show how cultural knowledge is understood and applied in practice. A thorough description of the data used in this book will be given in the chapter on methodology.

This book aims to open avenues for viewing cultural knowledge from new perspectives. The results shall help those who conceptualize, teach, study and adopt, meaning researchers, trainers and students of cultural knowledge respectively. This book attempts to make them reflect on the concept and perhaps improve on it. If cultural knowledge will be used as extensively in the future as it has been so far, this book shall particularly be of interest for those who teach and acquire the knowledge in order to stimulate continuous dialogue and learning regarding the phenomenon.

A number of companies, mainly Western, intend to prepare their employees for situations where they interact with others who belong to foreign cultures. The idea of providing cultural knowledge in the framework of ICT is supposed to help these people get acquainted with the unfamiliar cultural setting and therefore "get to know" the cultural background of people they will interact with. But what does culture actually mean? Since Hofstede and his approach will be of central interest for this book, his definition is herby cited:

> Culture is "the collective programming of the mind which distinguishes the members of one group or category of people from another" (Hofstede 1991), p. 4).

Culture in his understanding is organized in groups that can be distinguished from each other according to their programmed patterns of behaviour. These specific patterns are taught to students of ICT in order to become aware of the differences between their own "programming" and that of other cultures.

Cultural knowledge aims to facilitate individuals to become familiar with other cultures. The knowledge gained shall help prevent miscommunication, conflict or failure in intercultural encounters (for example (Caligiuri et al. 2001), (Earley 1987), (Jaeger 1995)). Hence there is an interest to guarantee a smooth communication between individuals coming from different cultures. The central interest in this book examines the claim that cultural knowledge does not only increase comprehension but also fosters respect for other cultures and their members (Day 1998). Acquiring knowledge about cultural values and habits is regarded as the foundation for one to show respect as soon as (s)he is capable to see the culture from its "vantage point". "Non-respect" is defined as ignorance towards cultural differences. It is the intention of this book is to critically assess whether cultural knowledge contains respectful representations that contributes or prevents interactions based on respect for cultural differences. Hence, the book is guided by the following research question (RQ):

How does cultural knowledge represent cultures and how may this prevent rather than encourage interactions based on respect for cultural differences?

The RQ is composed of the following sub-questions:

What are the conditions that constitute the basis of cultural knowledge?

What does the post-colonial and Levinasian perspective on cultural knowledge reveal?

What are the consequences of interest for interactions based on respect?

In order to answer the RQ, the analysis of cultural knowledge will be mainly composed of three parts:

The first part will introduce cultural knowledge by describing its historical development and briefly explaining the contributions of the most important scholars. After which, the "dominant interpretation" (see deconstruction for explanation of this term) of cultural knowledge will be highlighted.

The second and main part focuses on the post-colonial perspective on cultural knowledge and outlines the limitations endemic to the discourse. The book will analyze how PCT's main arguments are reflected in cultural knowledge and outline the consequences accordingly in terms of the RQ.

The third part focuses on Levinasian ethics and analyzes how the philosophy of Levinas can inform the deconstruction of cultural knowledge. In that regard the book will particularly turn to two aspects that Levinas makes us aware of. On the basis of the post-colonial as well as the Levinasian perspective, a conclusion will drawn that reflects on the RQ investigated.

1.4   STRUCTURE OF THE BOOK

The overall structure of the book will be as follows:

Chapter 2 explains the methodology used in the study. This book will contribute to critical management research and employs deconstruction as a critical reading of cultural knowledge. The data gathered for this book will be described in this chapter. As well as how the data will be used to critically assess cultural knowledge.

Chapter 3 gives a cohesive overview regarding the literature on PCT and Levinas. The part on PCT contains a section on the suggested solutions of PCT-scholars that aim to deal with the main criticisms outlined. These theories represent important contributions of PCT that embody valuable ideas for a constructive engagement with cultural knowledge. By way of the outline, I aim to guide the reader of this book towards the approach introduced by Levinas. In that regard it shall once more become clear why Levinasian ethics makes an important contribution to the analysis of cultural knowledge and to the process of answering the RQ.

Chapter 4 addresses the analysis (deconstruction) of cultural knowledge. The historical development of cultural knowledge and its main contributors are introduced prior to actual analysis. Some initial remarks on the constitution of cultural knowledge and the discussion of the terms "understanding" and "respect" represent the starting point of the deconstruction.

The author applies firstly PCT in the deconstruction of cultural knowledge. The main points of consideration will be the following: PCT takes the view that the West has constructed "far-off" places, meaning very foreign cultures as being wild and undeveloped. It therefore portrayed them as a **threat** to the West. Further, PCT criticizes the tendency to structure the world in **binary oppositions** since they are highly influenced by a Western perception of reality. As a consequence, the voice of the Other has been silenced. Scientific Western research understands itself as a superior knowledge system while other knowledge systems or self-understandings are excluded or not even considered (Jack, Westwood 2006). The knowledge is therefore **one-sided**. Last but not least PCT indicates that Western knowledge creation has undergone processes of **homogenization and simplification** of the object it studies. The process of representation manipulates difficult and complex material into something that can easily be grasped and controlled (Cooper 1992). The book will discuss the consequence that such knowledge implies for individuals who have acquired it and what this means concerning the idea of interactions based on respect.

The book will next focus on Levinas and his philosophy on ethics. His approach will illustrate that (cultural) knowledge **replaces individual responsibility**. Further it creates **totalities** that represent a closed system and therefore a limited picture of reality. Levinasian ethics suggests a way on how one can relate to difference in an ethical way and build up a relationship with one's counterpart without falling into the "traps" of cultural knowledge.

In chapter 5 the main points of the book shall be briefly summarized and a conclusion will be drawn. The conclusion will also include a discussion of limitations on theory and methodology used. Further it will point to possibilities for future research.

2   Methodology

2.1   CRITICAL MANAGEMENT RESEARCH

In this part of the book all methodological considerations and the collection and analysis of qualitative data is outlined. In order to answer the RQ, the study adopts the critical approach in an attempt to make a contribution to critical management research.

Alvesson and Deetz have paid enormous attention to the research paradigm of critical management research in their book, "Doing Critical Management Research" (Alvesson, Deetz 1999). They also aimed to define the paradigm. However, they stated that there is no tight relationship between a particular theoretical framework and a certain methodology. Therefore Alvesson and Deetz proposed for critical management research

> "a relatively loose framework characterized by a set of comments, reflections and possible guidelines for qualitative management research with a critical edge."
> ((Alvesson, Deetz 1999), p. 2)

It is the purpose of critical research that frames the research paradigm. Critical research disrupts social reality in order to liberate it from certain dominant streams and to consequently encourage new ideas. The object of interest is usually contextualized in a wider framework so that asymmetrical relations in society are exposed. This book uses the "framework" of PCT and Levinasian ethics to analyze and discuss cultural knowledge in terms of the RQ.

Alvesson and Deetz see in management a significant interest to govern and manage. They stated that management as a concept and category presents a social construction, which has significantly been impacted in particular by history and political motives. The interest to control and govern has driven the development of knowledge – including cultural knowledge (Alvesson, Deetz 1999). Adorno et al. claimed in the 1970s that modern discourse favours technological rationality over social life and in that way accounts for the interest of a new dominant group (Adorno, Horkheimer & Cumming 1979). Hence it is the task of critical research to reflect on Western knowledge creation and discuss to what extent it contains exclusions, concealments and silenced voices. I will analyze how these aspects are reflected in cultural knowledge and in which way streams of power interests of Western management have influenced it.

Besides the mentioned points, the study will also look at the epistemological beliefs of functionalist research. Cultural knowledge accounts for this paradigm. It believes that nature of reality consists of stable patterns and natural cause-effect laws and can therefore be generalized. The ontological belief of critical research however sees the nature of reality influenced by a variety of social, cultural and economic streams (Voce 2004). Critical research brings restrictive structures to light. In doing so it challenges the key assumption of positivist research that believes knowledge can be put into systems, reoccurs in situations and is true for a large group of people. We will see throughout this book that cultural knowledge has been put in systems and is understood to be stable over time. This is due to the implicit requirement asking for fixation and systematization for the sake of control. Or to put it in Alvesson's and Deetz's words: powerful agents produce a "frozen social reality" in order to serve certain interests ((Alvesson, Deetz 1999), p. 5).

With reference to PCT and Levinasian ethics, I will engage in a "critical reading" of cultural knowledge in order to analyse the extent to which respectful representations are manifested and therefore contribute to interactions based on respect. For the analysis deconstruction is employed, particularly ethical deconstruction as introduced by Simon Critchley.

2.2   DECONSTRUCTION

This chapter will give an introduction to "deconstruction" as developed by the French philosopher Jacques Derrida (1930 – 2004). After which, "ethical deconstruction", which was introduced by Simon Critchley in his work, "The Ethics of Deconstruction" will be presented ((Critchley 1999), if not stated otherwise, his book presents the reference for all of the following explanations in this section). Critchley pays close attention to Derrida's theory of deconstruction. He considers the representation of an ethical demand as its ultimate claim since the goal and horizon towards which Derrida's work tends *is* ethics. His point of view will be explained throughout this section of the chapter. To understand this, deconstruction in the Derridian sense is first discussed.

Deconstruction interrupts and gains insights into a particular text in order to reveal its blind spots and therefore open it up to new perspectives. Alvesson and Deetz indicated that deconstruction pays attention to "the dominance of a particular unity or point of view over others" ((Alvesson, Deetz 1999), p. 143). It deals with the uncovering of oppositions and denies univocal forms of knowledge. A text is seen to be dependent on hierarchical, oppositional positions and deconstruction aims to loosen them up (Kelemen, Rumens

2008). The oppositional position this book intends to reveal is as follows: cultural knowledge claims to constitute the foundation for comprehending cultural differences. At the same time it presents itself as the foundation for respect for cultural differences. Understanding and respect are demonstrated to be in consensus with each other. However by deconstructing cultural knowledge it will be revealed that these are rather treated in hierarchical ways, meaning, one of them is ascribed more importance than the other. It will become obvious that there is what Alvesson and Deetz call "privileged understanding" (Alvesson, Deetz 1999). In the case of cultural knowledge this is accounted for by the comprehension of cultural differences for the sake of control. Respect turns into a "nice to have" attribute and is subordinated to the former.

Deconstruction does not point at an ultimate truth, but rather strives to make the author aware of the limits of his role (Derrida, Habermas & Thomassen 2006). It is opened through reading that consists mainly of two steps: first, as Derrida explains, it aims to depict a "dominant interpretation" in a text. In the case of cultural knowledge and in reference to the RQ, the dominant interpretation accounts for the idea that cultural knowledge represents cultures in a way that constitutes the foundation for understanding *and* at the same time respect for cultural difference. Section 4.2 will explain the "dominant interpretation" and how it is assumingly taken care of, meaning how cultural knowledge is composed to represent a foundation for respect. Furthermore multiple contexts need to be taken into consideration in order to understand the dominant interpretation. In this regard, I will particularly inquire into how the historical development and corporate environment and its corresponding conditions have led to the way cultural knowledge has been conceptualized.

The second step reveals "blind spots" within the dominant interpretation that have been "silenced" so far. Critchley further takes the view that deconstruction sees a point of otherness within a text. The latter is deconstructed in order to reveal that the point of otherness nonetheless exists. It has simply been concealed. Hence deconstruction does not point at a new ultimate truth, it rather discloses a point of otherness. In this book the earlier mentioned term "blind spot" will be applied in order to depict the point of otherness. The revealed blind spots ultimately destabilize the stability of the dominant interpretation. The blind spots revealed to open the discourse on cultural knowledge are limitations outlined by PCT and Levinas. I will discuss the respective consequences for the individual who studies cultural knowledge in order to assess how the dominant interpretation is affected by the limitations of the concept.

This book does not precisely focus on the deconstruction of one text but on a concept and discourse. In particular cultural dimensions as introduced by Hall, Hofstede and Trompenaars will be analyzed. In addition, the study will refer to scholars who have discussed the purpose of cultural knowledge. This needs to be done since the knowledge cannot explain its purpose by itself. Thus the concept analyzed consists of more than one "text". It is the conviction here that a proper deconstruction will still be possible since they have been composed in the same way and aim for the same goals.

It is important to note that deconstruction does not come along with the denial of the dominant interpretation. It aims to challenge its stability in the first place, but does not question its existence per se. To put it in the context of this book: the dominant interpretation of cultural knowledge claims that it presents a foundation for understanding *and* respect at the same time. To challenge this interpretation does not involve the abrogation of the idea to deliver some sort of support (foundation) to increase understanding and develop respect for cultural differences. Most of the people interviewed in the study confirmed that some kind of help towards an understanding of other cultures is needed. However the point of deconstruction is to reveal how cultural knowledge has aimed to represent the foundation for encounters based on respect, but has derogated the same by deciding on particulars ways over others. Johnson clarifies:

> "Deconstruction is not synonymous with 'destruction', however. It is in fact much closer to the original meaning of the word 'analysis' itself, which etymologically means 'to undo' - a virtual synonym for 'to de-construct'" ((Johnson 1981), p.5)

Hence by deconstructing cultural knowledge, I do not bring "destruction" to the idea of delivering support. Despite all the effort to delve beneath a concept's surface and point at the "blind spots", there is still sympathy for the text (Kelemen, Rumens 2008). Deconstruction merely opens a text for blind spots that have undergone dissimulation or appropriation by a logo-centric text. It therefore does not aim to list criticisms that completely overrule the dominant interpretation.

Simon Critchley and his ideas on *ethical* deconstruction are hereby presented. He takes the view that deconstructive reading demands responsibility. It represents an ethical demand towards the reader of texts who "applies" deconstruction. Hence, me as the reader of cultural knowledge am encouraged to make sure that the patterns of my reading have an ethical structure. Ethics is therefore incorporated in reading and not a potential result of deconstruction. What this implies is reflected in Critchley's understanding of ethics. Here he refers to Levinas' conceptualization of the term. A thorough introduction to Levinasian ethics is given in the literature review. In order to understand what his approach means for the idea of deconstruction, here a few points are highlighted: Levinasian ethics frames ethics as first philosophy, meaning that it is prior to ontology. By placing ethics prior to any nature of things, Levinas does not, however, reject ontology. The same applies for the deconstruction in this book since it does not intend to overcome the idea of delivering support for intercultural encounters. Rather it gives room for the discussion of its limits. Ethics unfolds in the process of interrupting ontology in its claim to account for universality and absolute vision.

Derrida frames the process of deconstruction as "critical reading". Critchley suggests the term "clotural reading" for his approach of *ethical* deconstruction. It is the same process as critical reading and also occurs as double reading (dominant interpretation and blind spots). However it includes the question of ethics. Ethical deconstruction similarly searches for a point of otherness (blind spot) within a text. As it aims to create consciousness of and respect for the other, it also pays respect to the dominant interpretation. This means that it preserves the matter a text is composed for.

Deconstruction is merely interested in pointing to the vulnerability of a text/concept in order to enable ways towards new perspectives. It is a form of critique and analyzes,

> "an understanding, which is achieved without full consideration of alternative discourses and guiding principles of social life" ((Alvesson, Deetz 1999), p. 144).

Hence, it acts as an advocate for alternative discourses and guiding principles of social life. In this book deconstruction serves to promote the principle of respect. This is accomplished by revealing a hierarchical disparity in cultural knowledge that does not give the same importance to respect as well as to understanding for the sake of control.

A few words on the dilemma, deconstruction entails: if the critical reader seeks to point at otherness (alterity) in a text, (s)he needs to communicate, possibly write down what (s)he intends to say. But as soon as (s)he puts it into words, something is constituted, which does not respect alterity anymore. Deconstruction reflects the desire to always make alterity possible; ideally there is no final argument or absolute vision. The same accounts for me as the author of this book, as my arguments and conclusions may appear to be final. However, in terms of (ethical) deconstruction none of my words can be considered final. Thus, the possibility of deconstruction is challenged since it is burdened with a methodological problem. Despite these concerns I will attempt to employ deconstruction since it will be of great help in this book in dealing with the RQ.

2.3   DATA COLLECTION

This section gives an overview on the data collected that served to answer the RQ. Before I describe the data used in this research in detail, the structure of the actual deconstruction in this book shall be explained in order to clarify *how* the data is used. The deconstruction of cultural knowledge will comprehend five sections, each of them focusing on one potential limitation. Each section first describes a PCT- or Levinasian argument. Afterwards cultural knowledge will be analyzed according to the argument posed in order to see how the former mirrors it. Then excerpts are quoted from the interviews to illustrate the argument, meaning to show how the interviewees mirror the argument posed by PCT or Levinas. Thus, the quotes themselves will not be deconstructed. These only serve as illustrations. It has to be noted that the book does not aim to explore any new insights by looking at the interviews/ questionnaires. They mainly serve as a means to see whether the arguments or limitations have analogies in "reality". The deconstruction leads to conclusions on the consequences of the limitations for the individual who studies cultural knowledge.

To support the process of deconstruction, data in two forms is used: first, cultural knowledge itself presents an important part of the data because of the study's concern for its content and conceptualisation. In this regard the study will particularly focus on the features of cultural knowledge introduced by Edward T. Hall, Geert Hofstede and Fons Trompenaars. These represent the most important research in the field of cultural knowledge extensively taught in ICT ((Brislin, Yoshida 1994), (Morris, Robie 2001)). An introduction to their works is presented in section 4.2. The study will also refer to authors that have commented on the purpose of cultural knowledge since the knowledge itself cannot reveal what it aims to accomplish. In this regard, I refer to texts and handbooks on intercultural communication, cultural competence and ICT.

Qualitative data from semi-structured interviews and short questionnaires were also collected. The semi-structured interviews were conducted with employees of a Danish pharmaceutical company who are exposed to an intercultural working environment. I also spoke to a consultant who composes ICT-concepts. Only one of the employees interviewed took part in an ICT and was therefore familiar with all the theoretical concepts on cultural knowledge. In conversations with those who were not familiar with cultural knowledge such as Hofstede's research, I tried to find out if and how gathering that type of knowledge would have helped them. The interview with the consultant served the interest of understanding how ICT is conceptualized and the role that cultural knowledge plays here, meaning, why it is taught and which goal it tries to achieve. The arguments of the consultant are therefore quoted in consonance with scholars who have discussed the purpose of cultural knowledge.

In addition, I asked five former fellow students to fill out a short questionnaire in order to get impressions on their experiences with cultural knowledge. Their answers were regarded as useful since all of the students studied cultural knowledge at university. Furthermore, they have at least once been exposed to intercultural settings during their studies abroad and work today in international companies. Using a questionnaire, I tried to collect information showing how cultural knowledge is applied to make sense of cultural differences. The questionnaires also revealed examples that reflect the practice of cultural knowledge.

The interviews/questionnaires were decoded with the aim of identifying illustrations for the arguments posed by PCT and Levinas. It was found that statements on the goal which cultural knowledge intends to achieve to be related to the constitution of cultural differences as a threat. Examples of significant cultural differences displayed binaries and subliminal interpretations. Other examples regarding how cultural knowledge has helped in intercultural settings illustrated homogenization and simplification. A particular example revealed how, in the Levinasian sense, individual responsibility is replaced by knowledge. The points of Levinas on the aspects of a totality refer to the post-colonial perspective on homogenization and simplification and the respective interview/questionnaire quotes (section 4.3.1.3).

The interviewees will remain anonymous. However the interviews and questionnaires were coded in order to allocate quotes. The former was marked with the letter "I" and the latter with "Q". "I4" refers to the interview conducted with the consultant. I aim to give a voice to each interview or questionnaire at least once in order to avoid dependency on one particular set of data and increase the validity of my arguments.

2.4   VALIDITY AND RELIABILITY OF THE DATA USED

In this book PCT and Levinasian ethics are strong explanatory elements for the limitations of cultural knowledge. However, it is important to choose specific data on cultural knowledge to investigate the extent to which it reflects the limitations outlined. In this regard, the study depends on secondary data such as concepts of cultural knowledge and the discourse on the issue in academic articles that have particularly explained its purpose. Further, the interviews and questionnaire represent primary data and will increase the validity of the final conclusions.

One major limitation occurred with respect to the interviews conducted with employees of a Danish pharmaceutical company. Since only one interviewee had participated in an ICT, the content of the other interviews were only helpful to a certain degree. All of the interviewees who filled out the questionnaires were familiar with cultural knowledge relevant for this book. However, the trainings that the interviewees participated in were all conducted during their time at university a few years ago. Thus, to increase the validity of this research interviews with participants of ICT that are conducted in business environments, could be of high interest. Interviews with participants who have recently taken part in a training and shortly afterwards went abroad where they applied the knowledge learnt are particularly interesting. I tried to get in contact with such people, but encountered major problems since the consultant interviewed in the study was not allowed to forward any contact details due to data protection and confidentiality. The companies contacted that conducted trainings on cultural knowledge mainly offered culture-specific trainings where participants learn the "do's and don'ts" but do not learn about more general issues regarding cultural differences in intercultural communication.

Another aspect is the reliability of the data. It concerns "the extent to which similar observations would be made or conclusions reached by other researchers or whether there is transparency in how sense was made from the raw data" ((Saunders, Lewis & Thornhill 2007), p. 609). Since the reliability of qualitative data is difficult to measure, triangulation is commonly used to deal with this issue. Easterby-Smith et al define the term as "using different kinds of measure or perspectives in order to increase the confidence in the accuracy of observations ((Easterby-Smith, Thorpe & Jackson 2008), p. 334). The analysis in this book is primarily based on secondary data such as concepts and academic contributions. However, primary data was also used from interviews and questionnaires. This accounts for the inclusion of multiple sources and triangulation was assured.

The next chapter presents a profound introduction to PCT and is followed by a thorough introduction to Levinas and his philosophy on ethics.

3 Literature Review

This chapter introduces PCT and Levinasian ethics in order to build a theoretical foundation for the deconstruction of cultural knowledge. It highlights the main arguments followed by the presentation of examples that demonstrate how scholars have "applied" these ideas to investigate current issues in the (International) Business field.

3.1 Post-Colonial Theory

3.1.1 Historical Development

PCT has established itself as part of academic discourse, in particular in social science. A definition of PCT was given in the introduction. To reiterate this, Westwood et al. are cited who stated that PCT refers to the discussion of "power asymmetries, imbalances and repressions" in the representation of cultural identities (Westwood, Jack 2007), p. 247). It refers to colonialism since it concerns itself with the cultural effects of colonization (Ashcroft, Griffiths & Tiffin 1998). Despite PCT's relation to historical terms, post-colonial argumentation is also used today as a way to criticize the imperialistic tendencies of International Management (IM) practices. PCT therefore also describes the

> "continuing reproduction of neo-colonial structures […] as part of Western management techniques and ways of knowing" ((Jack, Lorbiecki 2003), p. 213).

Thus PCT is also employed to analyze, assess and critically reflect on contemporary issues. Young stated that the effects of colonialism are still present in cultural and material ways, especially regarding today's economic power distribution and capitalism (Young 2000). In this book cultural knowledge will be analyzed in order to come to conclusions on how it reflects such aspects. And further how this influences representations of cultures and what this implies for intercultural encounters based on respect.

The term "PCT" was originally used to denote the historical era after colonial rule. However since the 1970s it represents a discourse, which critically investigates influences of colonial power. It therefore comprises much more than only a historical period. Consequently the prefix "post" has been exposed to many debates: Mishra and Hodge cited that the term points at progress which did not necessarily occur in the way described since various forms of colonialism led to different kinds of de-colonisation (Mishra, Hodge 1994). Mc Leod supported the above-mentioned aspect of the discourse's topicality and claims that post-colonialism is not the same as "after colonialism" since discourse from the colonial era is still with us today and the term cannot clearly be segregated from the era of colonialism (Mc Leod 2000). In this book PCT is used to analyze cultural knowledge in order to find an answer to the RQ. To put it in Prasad's words: PCT represents the channel to the "radical and ethically informed critique of Western modernity" (Prasad 2003), p. 33). By employing clotural reading of cultural knowledge and thereby engaging PCT, this book contributes to the critique of Western modernity.

The most important contributors of post-colonial discourse are Edward W. Said, Homi K. Bhabha and Gayatri C. Spivak (a detailed description of their work will follow in this section of the chapter). They have particularly been concerned with the colonies' discursive power (Ashcroft, Griffiths & Tiffin 1998). The scholars' interest focused on whether aspects of colonialism are still prevalent and particularly how they influenced contemporary identities and realities. The process of colonialism is seen as a dramatic intervention into the culture of the colonized: the colonizer conquers a country and in order to secure power imposes his culture upon the colonized by changing and destroying the local culture. Hence it is of less importance how they dealt with the colonized physically or how governmental power was established. It is rather of interest how the colonizer clearly distinguished colonised people from themselves in terms of habits, values and behaviours and therefore rendered them as being "other", being different. However, as outlined by Westwood's definition of PCT, the criticism of post-colonial scholars pointed to the deployment of such resources to establish and maintain power asymmetries. Kwek further stated that PCT aims to reveal power systems that favour certain representations and silence others (Kwek 2003). These power systems are of interest when it comes to an inquiry of justice regarding the representation of cultures in cultural knowledge.

3.1.2 Main Arguments

One main argument of PCT is the assumed but not existing neutrality in cultural representations (Jack, Westwood 2006). PCT-scholars, particularly Edward W. Said, claimed that cultural representations are rife with binaries, which structure the world into polarities. Said introduced his main ideas in the book "Orientalism" (see (Said 1978)). He stated that the Orient is a "cultural production" in opposition to reflection on the given reality. (Jack, Westwood 2006). The Orient is located, structured and regulated through "knowledge" and described as being wild and exotic. This however is only possible by referring to the "modern" occidental world. In that way, post-colonial scholars indicated that the Orient is rendered as a threat and inferior to the modern Western world ((Mc Leod 2000), (Rhodes, Westwood 2007)).

So, how is this exactly done? Colonized cultures are framed into categories, which are defined by Western terms. Consequently binary polarisation occurs where Orient and Occident exist in opposition and are made meaningful in reference to each other (Mc Leod 2000). PCT regards the self-defined representations imposed upon reality and the Other as a mean to serve the purpose of control (for example (Kwek 2003), (Mishra, Hodge 1994), (Munshi, McKie 2001)). If these interests influence knowledge creation, the latter does not reflect a neutral picture of reality. It merely serves the interest to structure the world and to secure power.

Said's theory has not been immune to criticism either: Mc Leod indicated that *Orientalism* ignored resistances by both sides and totalized assumptions which cover a long historical period (Mc Leod 2000). His contributions are nonetheless of high importance to the PCT as they describe the Occident's interest in gathering information and "produce" cultures instead of getting "real" knowledge about the Other.

PCT has also brought forward the argument that knowledge creation has undergone homogenization and simplification. These processes lead to a codified representation of cultures and yet again serve the interest of control and power (Munshi, McKie 2001). Only if other (colonized) cultures are represented in a clear way then control becomes possible since one has a brief idea of how "they" work. It is therefore less of interest whether representations represent an accurate and reliable picture of reality. As long as codified systems lead to control, homogenization and simplifications seem acceptable.

Further the argument of silenced voices has been raised by PCT-scholars: excluding and silencing the Other in the process of generating cultural representations leads to a simplified picture where essentialisms prevail. The consequence is a limited picture, which however can more easily be engaged (Kwek 2003). The Other is silenced and only left to fit and mould of the imposed representations. These representations are constructed of and for the West (Jack, Westwood 2006).

The discourse on PCT is therefore closely related to power issues. Many scholars have declared that cultural categories and identities result out of power strategies (Prasad 2003), (Vaara et al. 2005), (Westwood 2006). The mentioned aspects will be used in the analysis of cultural knowledge to see whether interests of power and control have influenced the way cultural knowledge is conceptualized and in what way.

2.1.3   Suggested Solutions

This section presents solutions suggested by post-colonial scholars in order to deal with the above-mentioned criticisms. In this respect, the book particularly considers the works of Bhabha and Spivak. They suggested to strive for understanding in the actual encounters instead of pursuing knowledge creation prior to the actual interaction. All of the mentioned approaches have one commonality though: they strive for "real", justified and "pure" knowledge about the (culturally foreign) counterpart. They, however, differ regarding the way this shall be accomplished.

Said saw no justice in how other cultures (the Orient) were represented (Said 1978). The solution often given by post-colonial scholars is the creation of space where the Other can "speak back" (for example (Hickling-Hudson 2003), (Jack, Westwood 2006), (Kwek 2003)). However, uncontested truths are not achieved by simply including "native" descriptions since this would "repeat the error of attributing a descriptive neutrality to social actors" (Jack, Westwood 2006), p. 488). Thus "free" or "pure" knowledge seems an impossible undertaking since "native" descriptions nonetheless need translation into one's own words and categories.

A further suggestion is concerned with simplification and fixation of cultural representations. Bjerregaard et al. saw a static view of culture that did not pay any attention to contexts such as power relationships as well as social and organizational environments (Bjerregaard, Lauring & Klitmøller 2009). They claimed that more aspects other than static values influence culture. A solution is seen in shifting the understanding of culture from culture-as-code to culture-in-context. However it seems that Bjerregaard et al. only widened the scope and added more factors that need to be observed in order to understand culture and context. In so doing one gets a better understanding of the particular culture. The observation is nevertheless done from a one-sided (western) point of view. Consequently Bjerregaard et al. still aimed at understanding cultures without being aware of one-sidedness.

If there are no neutral representations, do we have to conclude that any process of gathering knowledge about cultures should be abandoned? Bhabha and Spivak have given a different spin on the topic. They shifted the attention from scientific knowledge gathering towards the actual interaction where they see the formation of "knowledge".

Bhabha agreed in his book "The Location of Culture" that colonial discourse aimed to construe the colonized nationalities as being "degenerate types on the basis of racial origin" ((Bhabha 1994), p.70). By this means power is justified and established. However his main criticism pointed at stereotypes - the main outcome of such processes as he claimed. Bhabha defined them as

> "form of knowledge and identification that vacillates between what is always 'in place', already known, and something that must be anxiously repeated" ((Bhabha 1994), p.66).

He saw the central problem in the fixation of cultural identities (of the West as well as the Non-West). However he recognized that fixation is crucial to the process of colonization since it is a key contributor to the construction of otherness or the "production of culture" as it was also outlined by Said. In that way the colonized or culturally Other becomes predictable and manageable. The stereotype represents the main discourse tool in that matter. And in order to be repeatable across changing historical and discursive situations, the stereotype needs to exceed any empirical proof. As a matter of fact, stereotypes cannot be proven and do not need to be proven. This presents ambivalence, which is one of its key characteristics that establish fixations. It is rather through their constant repetition and the creation of further stereotypes that manifestation takes place.

Bhabha did not intend to demonstrate the negative or positive side of colonial discourse. He was mainly interested in the ineffectiveness of stereotypes. He suggested an alternative approach to the fixation of cultural identities. This approach asks for the recognition of complexity and a "space of hybridity", a space within which cultural identities are negotiated. Following Bhabha's ideas, cultural identities are not formed through knowledge creation *about* the Other, but in interaction *with* the Other. Thus what is needed is a different stake on the topic that moves from the observation of the Other towards a mediated interaction. It is the latter that contributes to the understanding and formation of cultural identities. In Bhabha's understanding cultural identities are negotiated and formed in interaction. Through the relation to the counterpart's otherness (something that cannot be rendered and is beyond categories), one is called into being since there is nothing like an independent self (that is comprehendible without the "mirror" of the other person) just as there is no absolute Other. Any kind of knowledge about the Other, which was gathered before the interaction, would therefore disavow alterity. Ashcroft et al. defined the term "alterity" as "the state of being other or different" ((Ashcroft, Griffiths & Tiffin 1998), p. 11). Since there is no absolute Other stereotypes are not capable of explaining in a reliable way how persons are alike. Bhabha was particularly interested in demonstrating that stereotypes are ineffective. Rhodes and Westwood have supported him in his argument and stated that the stereotype is destabilized throughout the interaction since individuals may not fulfil it (Rhodes, Westwood 2007). Thus we cannot rely on stereotypes and need an approach that denies pre-knowledge and points at the direct interaction with the counterpart.

Bhabha's theory does not agree with Said in the following: he questioned any kind of "fixed" knowledge and did not focus on neutrality of knowledge. He went one step further and stated that any knowledge will not live up to its aim of mirroring the Other since the fixation that is inherent in stereotypes will be challenged in interaction. However even though Said and Bhabha have different points of departure, Bhabha's argument appears nonetheless to be another quest for the abandonment of pre-knowledge. His reflections on stereotypes shed light on their limitations. By questioning their effectiveness he challenged the idea of representation in general. Rather he directed attention to the actual interaction. Bhabha further indicated how stereotypes disavow alterity. Hence he ascribed not only ineffectiveness but also unethical tendencies to the concept of stereotypes. The Other is confined to categories and stereotypes, while otherness that does not comply is ignored.

Spivak disagreed with Bhabha on the question whether representation and the process of gathering knowledge about other cultures should be refused. She demonstrated that "to refuse to represent a cultural Other is salving your conscience, and allowing you not to do any homework" ((Spivak 1988), p. 62-63). To a certain extent Spivak agrees with Bhabha. She argued that the Other contained an "inaccessible blankness", which cannot simply be "observed" or even comprehended. She also stated that alterity or otherness can never be accessed completely (Spivak 1993b). Hence Spivak's "inaccessible blankness" agrees with Bhabha's non-existing absolute Other.

Even if there are definite limits regarding the possibilities of investigation, Spivak nevertheless supported the view that representation should not be avoided in general. Essentialist categories (e.g. woman, race) are permissible and the "production of theory is in fact a very important practice that is worlding the world in a certain way" ((Spivak 1990), p. 24). This seems to be a starting point when it comes to the interaction with the counterpart. So, are we back to categories and stereotypes that are set up from a one-sided point of view? The answer to this question does not seem a strict "yes" or "no", it is rather an inquiry into how we can represent the Other in an ethical way where we do not fall into the trap of fixed (unethical) stereotypes. According to the theory/literature introduced so far, what is needed is to find a way that does not ignore the observer's background, but at the same time represents the Other in a respectful, thus ethical way. Rhodes and Westwood saw this requirement answered by Spivak (Rhodes, Westwood 2007). The particularity of her approach can be seen in the way she understood the process of information gathering. She referred to Derrida who rejected allowing the Other speak for himself. He took the view that we should refer to an "interior voice that is the voice of the other in us" ((Spivak 1988), p. 89). This voice calls the "quite-other" (tout autre) in us. It is important to her that one learns how to learn from the Other and is willing to "unlearn" any prejudices (Kapoor 2004). Thus some kind of essentialism and theory is needed to understand the world and human beings. It is only from there that one can "learn to unlearn prejudices" and therefore clear the way in order to "learn to learn" from the Other. Essentialisms are therefore only one step on the way to an ethical relationship. Nonetheless does one always have to be aware of their strategic status and regard them as a means on the way to liberation and not repression (Rhodes, Westwood 2007).

To sum it up, post-colonial scholars have suggested allowing the Other "speak back" and/or to include more factors in dealing with one-sidedness as well as homogenization and simplification respectively. These ideas merely strive to achieve neutral knowledge that reflects reality the most. However despite the inclusion of more voices and factors, Spivak's theory of "inaccessible blankness" and Bhabha's argument on the instability of cultural stereotypes still remain.

The introduction to this book outlined the interest in intercultural encounters based on respect where respect is understood as a tolerant attitude and the difference of the counterpart is given room and an equal right to exist (see also 4.2). The next section focuses on Emmanuel Levinas and his philosophy on ethics. He introduced a theory suggesting how one can become capable to ethically relate to difference. To justify the usefulness of his approach to the book, I argue the following:
The difference between the approach of PCT with that of Levinas is rooted in what it ultimately aims to achieve: while PCT discussed the best way to represent cultures and to

gather knowledge, Levinas was interested in an ethical self-other-relationship and more importantly, an ethical relation to difference. Most post-colonial scholars did not participate in the discussion of how the actual *interaction* with the counterpart could be approached in an ethical way. It was Spivak who solely introduced an idea of an ethical relation to difference, of an ethical encounter with the Other. However her approach still contributed to the search of knowledge. Hence her focus was not on ethics in the actual relationship with the Other but on an ethical way of gathering knowledge.

Levinas however, considered the relationship to the Other to be *always* an ethical one. And ethics to his mind is "first philosophy". This implies that the decision whether categories/knowledge is used is already an ethical one. One has the choice to make the Other into the same or approach her/him in another way (Muhr 2008a). This decision has implications for the self-Other relationship and I would like to point at them by reflecting Levinas' ideas on cultural knowledge. He is therefore less concerned with an ethical way of gathering knowledge as suggested by PCT. Rather he points to the implications of the general process of knowledge gathering for interactions based on respect. As stated earlier, the main merit of Levinas consists of a reminder regarding the importance of an ethical self-Other-relationship.

3.2   Emmanuel Levinas and his Philosophy on Ethics

3.2.1   Life and Key Writings

The French post-war philosopher Emmanuel Levinas (1906 - 1995) was deeply concerned with our way of experiencing the Other. Levinasian ethics suggests that our relationship to other human beings is always of an ethical nature since we have to make a decision as to whether we let the Other be other or use knowledge to make the Other into the same (Muhr 2008a). Levinas' ideas will be explained in detail throughout this section of the chapter.

Levinas was born in Lithuania 1906, but obtained French citizenship in 1930. His life was coloured by a Jewish background and his experiences in the German military prisoners' camp during the Second World War (he was not sent to a concentration camp since he was part of the French army). Levinas began his philosophical studies in Strasbourg in 1924. In 1928, he moved to Freiburg where he studied under Edmund Husserl and Martin Heidegger for two years. After earning a doctorate at the Université de Poitiers in Paris,

Levinas started teaching at several French universities from the 1960s onwards. It is remarkable that his work - despite the tragic experiences in his life - does not express any anger nor hate. It is rather a claim for humanity and compassion (see (Critchley, Bernasconi 2002) for an extended introduction to Levinas). Levinas' two books "Totality and Infinity" (1969) and "Otherwise than Being or Beyond Essence" (1981) are essential contributions to Western philosophy. Further he reflects in his book "Humanism of the Other" (1972) three essays on humanism as well as recent philosophical debates. Here he, as Cohen highlighted in the introduction to the book, "represent[s] the full height and maturation of his thought" ((Levinas 2003), p. XXVI).

3.2.2 Main Arguments

3.2.2.1 Levinasian Ethics

Levinas and his philosophy are often referred to as "Levinasian ethics". He pointed out though that his approach does not aim to provide a normative concept, which teaches human beings precisely what to do. But what is the difference between a normative approach and ethics? Pieper understands ethics as a science, which sets the criteria that serve to decide whether an action is a moral one (Pieper 2009). It does not give advice on specific (moral) actions on how to achieve a good goal. Rather it discusses the formal criteria, which do not tell us *what* is good but *how* we judge something being good. Consequently ethics does not evaluate single actions. It discusses on a meta-level how actions are morally judged and is therefore distanced to the object itself. Pieper further indicates that freedom of the self represents a crucial foundation of human actions since it is only through freedom that we can set our own rules and follow them voluntarily. One then achieves a state of morality as a consequence of arising commitment. Two aspects limit each individual's freedom though: first, un-reversible facts are beyond one's power. Secondly, by the freedom of others that should not be affected by someone embracing one's own freedom.

Levinas' philosophy challenges the concept of freedom: he asks for an infinite responsibility towards the Other that has the power (and allowance) to confine any kind of freedom and spontaneity of the ego. The responsibility for the Other is more important and prior to "my" freedom (Critchley 1999). Cohen refers to Levinasian ethics when he says "to be human is to care for the other above oneself" (introduction to (Levinas 2003), p. XXXIV). Hence Levinas supports the second limitation outlined in the previous paragraph. He stated that the individual's freedom should never confine the other person's freedom. However he goes one step further and debates that the infinite responsibility for the Other is allowed to confine one's own freedom. This act represents the realization of humanity, which is "constituted in the moral overcoming of the natural reflexivity of being, its recurrence, its selfishness" (introduction to (Levinas 2003), p. XXXIV). Here reciprocity is not expected.

Does that mean that he argues against autonomous freedom? His approach challenged the concept, but merely in the sense that Levinas understands it as "ethical freedom" (Rosenthal 2003). In his approach a new form of freedom is given way: freedom through acceptance of moral transcendence and infinite responsibility towards the Other. Ethical freedom is realized when otherness is allowed to confine (autonomous) freedom since the Other calls for responsibility. Rosenthal further stated that freedom has been understood as the opposite of obligation (Rosenthal 2003). It constitutes a state of being that is not confined to any rules and norms. Levinasian ethics however positions responsibility at the centre of the self-Other-relationship. In that way it becomes a central part of our ethical freedom. Hence the freedom of the self is not in contradiction to the presence of the Other. The presence rather needs to be regarded as a "present", which enables us to realize an ethical/responsible freedom (Scott no year).

Even if the care for the Other exceeds the care for the self, Levinasian ethics does not claim that the Other needs to be treated like a god-like being. Bauman pointed out that the Other has no power over "me" since this would reject an idea of the "face". Further it would regard the counterpart as an ontological being (Bauman 2004). "Face" was defined by Levinas as "the way in which the Other presents himself, exceeding the idea of the Other in me" ((Levinas 1969), p. 21). If the Other is treated as an ontological being past and present will gain importance. The Other in turn gains power over the self where a force influences the self's behaviour. The "face" on the other hand expresses merely an authority without any force (Bauman 2004). At the same time – and in order to account for infinite responsibility - a willingness to listen before the Other has spoken is crucial. Power or any kind of force of the Other is not in the Levinasian sense.

Levinas' approach is therefore rather an inquiry into the understanding of ethics. As seen in the previous paragraph, he uses the term "ethics", but introduces a totally different spin on the topic. Derrida indicated that "when Levinas speaks of ethics – I wouldn't say that this has nothing in common with what has been covered […], ethics is wholly other, and yet it is the same word" (Derrida in (Critchley 1999), p.16).

Levinas understands ethics as "first philosophy". As Derrida stated, it represents a "wholly other" approach because Levinas positions it before ontology and epistemology. Since the Other is given the authority to interrupt our (autonomous) freedom, responsibility is positioned prior to being. It is therefore also prior to ontology, the science of being. The same applies for epistemology, the philosophical theory of knowledge. Due to the central importance of ethics in Levinas' philosophy, it becomes the condition for knowledge and is therefore prior to epistemology. Because responsibility is prior to being and ethics prior to knowledge, Levinas' philosophy or Levinasian ethics is understood as more important than knowledge or epistemology. It should always have priority. Thus the importance ascribed to knowledge in concepts such as cultural knowledge does not coincide with a Levinasian perspective.

So how is the mentioned responsibility called into action? Bevan and Corvellec stated that it does not arise from the individual's behaviour and knowledge as a moral object (Bevan, Corvellec 2007). It is part of our individuality, prior to anything and does not need to be "called" into action. Responsibility is therefore not a consequence of rationality; it is prior to it (Aasland 2004). Nonetheless do we have to become aware of our inherent responsibility and activate it in our encounter with the Other. Only then the individual "re-sponds" to the infinite demand and "call" of the Other (Bevan, Corvellec 2007). Further (s)he is able to respond to the singularity of the situation (Jeanes, Muhr 2010). Since the call of the Other is always "to come", responsibility has to be infinite. Thus it will never be good enough to cope with the never-ending and always existing call of the Other (Levinas 1981).

Wild outlined in his introduction to Levinas' book "Totality and Infinity" that language is the only way one can coexist with the counterpart without "affecting" otherness (Levinas 1969). The glance of the Other's face forces me to respond. Only if a *responsible* answer is given, communication takes places where my world is put into words and offered to the Other. A self-Other-relation develops as a consequence, however without endangering the autonomy of both sides. Since the self refrains from treating the Other as an object of interpretation, everyone can speak her/his mind freely. That does not mean though that it is simply enough to let everybody speak at will; Levinas takes the view that we need to be able to respond. In that way we become responsible and take the Other seriously (Levinas 1969). Communication is not a passive, but an active act where we interact with the Other. Only in that way is one able to give room to diversity of dialogue and dynamic growth.

Related to the aspect of communication is Levinas' clear distinction between the Saying and the Said. Levinas encouraged us to focus on the Saying. By doing so one can live up to the infinite responsibility towards the Other without reducing it to any kind of signs or theories (the Said). The Saying can therefore be understood as the active, open communication to the Other. It has not previously been influenced (and limited) by anything, which is understood as "the Said". The Saying is prior to meaning and the "signifying antecedent to being" ((Bevan, Corvellec 2007), p. 216). It is "free" and therefore represents ethics since it can account for an ethical relationship to the Other. The Said on the other hand is related to ontology (Ricoeur 1997, in (Bevan, Corvellec 2007)). Only in the Saying do we find morality and justice since it lies prior to the Said and therefore gives room to the *Humanism of the Other* (Levinas 2003). The mentioned aspects are another claim for the rejection of anything, which confines the infinite responsibility and therefore real and ethical experience of the Other. Generosity and openness come into existence if nothing limits the experience of the Other. However we have to set the stage, because the Other cannot interrupt us if we do not give space to otherness.

The concept of infinity challenges Bhabha's argument that identities are formed in interaction through mirroring. Levinas however regards the self and Other as absolutely separated where neither engages in the being of the counterpart (Scott no year). He expects the individual to derive her/his meaning or identity only from her-/himself. If the self becomes dependent on the Other in its self-understanding though, the Other gains power. And, as outlined before, this is not in the Levinasian sense. Mirroring means understanding and – in Levinasian terms – a totality. Whether the goal of understanding is shifted towards the interaction and, according to Bhabha, assumed to give a "clearer" picture, does not matter in the Levinasian sense. He directs our attention towards infinity, which enables moral consciousness and consequently the self can welcome the Other (Scott no year). Even though Bhabha criticized the concept of stereotypes, his idea of a place of hybridity is not in accord with the Levinasian approach. It is (still) the strife for ultimate knowledge that influenced Bhabha's ideas. It should be clear by now that Levinasian ethics marks an inquiry into the general concept of the search for knowledge. Where does this leave us in the case of cultural knowledge? Functionalist knowledge about cultures does not only prevent justice of representation, it also does not live up to an ethical experience of the

Other in the Levinasian sense. As stated in the introduction, many corporations are concerned that their employees fail in intercultural interaction. They assume that cultural knowledge taught in ICT prepares them accordingly. That might be true to a certain extent. However factors such as justice of representation and ethics in the actual encounter with the Other are excluded or simply ignored here.

Following Levinasian ethics might seem like being hurled into something without knowing what to expect. And this is exactly what cultural knowledge aims to prevent. By teaching knowledge about foreign cultures and intercultural differences, it aims to support individuals in dealing with situations where unknown or unforeseen things might happen. Culture is understood as a source of irritation, which potentially makes interactions fail. In particular it is assumed that the counterparts do not understand each other in their cultural specificity. Levinas however claimed that we gain access to culture *through* our exposure to the Other. He further stated that:

> "Cultures are no longer obstacles that separate us from the essential and the intelligible; they are the paths by which we can reach it" (introduction to (Levinas 2003), p. XXIX).

Only through access can we understand what culture is about. Levinas pointed out that culture and symbols *do* offer us access to signification because "signification is not separate from the access leading to it" (introduction to (Levinas 2003), p. XXIX). It is therefore the exposure to culture and symbols itself that helps people make sense of it. Anything happening prior to that is not in accord with the Levinasian sense. However it is not only exposure but also access that is required. But how is access gained then? It becomes possible if room is given to otherness, which takes place in the face-to-face encounter with the Other. It is here where culture unfolds. Access means signification at the same time since it is part of the former. Thus to access signification, one has to acknowledge that knowledge ends where the complexity of otherness starts. Knowledge therefore cannot live up to signification. It is in the infinite responsibility which is prior to culture. Responsibility ultimately leads to access. And it is before the cultural expression where the *Humanism of the Other* is located.

This is reminiscent of Bhabha who advocated a space of hybridity in the interaction where he saw cultural identities take form. Bhabha and Levinas both agreed that one is only in the encounter able to comprehend the counterpart's characteristics. Levinas' main interest is however located in an ethical approach which represents the *precondition* for the experience of signification. Access and therefore signification are only gained if the Other is approached in an ethical way. Bhabha did not take ethics into account. He saw the interaction as an ideal situation to shape identities and learn about the Other. Hence, while Bhabha criticized stereotypes as being ineffective Levinas directed his criticism towards the non-existing moral imperative of symbols. He therefore focused on the opportunity to build up an ethical relationship with other individuals as well as the realization of the humanistic self.

Last but not least I turn to the problem of the "Third". Levinasian ethics and perhaps ethics in general represent a concept for particularly two human beings. Ethics can be taken cared of as long as one strives to show infinite responsibility towards the Other. However a dilemma occurs as soon as a third person enters the situation. The other Other, namely the Third, creates a tension (Bevan, Corvellec 2007). (S)he demands the same infinite responsibility as the Other. The responsibility is therefore doubled by the presence of the other Other, the Third. Bevan and Corvellec stated further that the re-doubling of responsibility lead to a concern of justice. Justice is fulfilled if the responsibility towards the Other is balanced with the demand of responsibility of all Others. Balance is achieved by measuring, comparing and setting priorities to bring justice to each single Other. These decisions are also of ethical nature since one is responsible for how (s)he decides in order to cause the least violations possible (Aasland 2007).

3.2.2.2 Levinas' Critique of Western Philosophy as an Ontology

One key term in Levinasian ethics is the "otherness" of the Other. Levinas stated that we have no choice but to acknowledge the Other as being other (Jeanes, Muhr 2010). However not only is the Other radical different, there is also something incomprehensible in the counterpart's otherness. That is to say that the Other will never be fully understood or "grasped.". (S)he is transcendent. People are limited in their understanding since their own categories are used to comprehend something that is "radical different". Hence something so different cannot be fully accounted for. Wild, who summarized Levinas' ideas in the introduction to his book "Totality and Infinity", explained that Levinas saw the consequence of the process described as the reduction of the Other into what he is not (introduction to (Levinas 1969)). In so doing one makes the Other into the same by placing him in her/his world. Wild further pointed out that Levinas understood human beings as either being able to see the counterpart as an extension of oneself or as something tremendously different. In the latter case manipulation of the object is needed. Later in his book Levinas brought forward the argument that

> "Western philosophy has most often been an ontology: a reduction of the other to the same by interposition of a middle and neutral term that ensures the comprehension of being." ((Levinas 1969), p. 43)

Thus if one refrains from "interposing middle and neutral terms", the Other is not reduced to the same and an original experience of the counterpart through unlimited openness becomes possible. Levinas understood that any interaction with the Other is an ethical one where openness to otherness is the key and the self is willing to be interrupted by the Other. Interruption means interrupting one's common sense and patterns of understanding (Muhr 2008b). Since the moral duty to let interruption happen is prior to the self, morality is prior to ontology.

Reflecting on Levinas' thoughts of transcendence brings the reader back to Spivak who saw an "inaccessible blankness" in the other person. Spivak however does not give up on the idea that even this blankness might become clear one day. Levinas would disagree at this point: he believed that difference is radical and infinite. Any attempt to understand could never live up to the counterpart's Otherness since it is not visible and cannot be put into categories: it is metaphysical and transcendent (Muhr 2008a).

It becomes clear at this point that ethics come to the fore and replace the search for "ultimate knowledge". If the Other is rendered in categories, infinite responsibility becomes impossible since the Other is confined to what he is not and openness to otherness is impeded. The comfort of existing norms and rules to guide the individual is denied to make sure that the individual lives up to her/his duty of infinite responsibility towards the Other (Bauman 2004).

As stated, categorization is fundamentally criticized from a Levinasian point of view. However it has been prevalent in history (in particular during colonization) and is still used today. Inherent here is the belief that unknown things represent a danger to established systems. In order to deal with potential "dangers", manipulation is considered necessary. In his way knowledge about the object of interest becomes a required precondition. Levinas understood such strategies as the idea of "totality", which stands for an "all-inclusive, panoramic view of all things" (introduction to (Levinas 1969), p.15). From a Levinasian point of view, however, a person has to give room to the counterpart and her/his difference without projecting any danger arising out of it. Only in that way can an ethical experience of the other person become possible.

By arguing for an ethical experience of the Other, Levinas did not only introduce a new understanding of ethics, but also a shift in justice. PCT pointed to injustice inherent in western knowledge. It was claimed that "fuller" and "more neutral" knowledge is needed. However if the philosophy of Levinas was followed, the point of departure occurs somewhere else: he does not ask for justice of representation but justice of our experience of the other. People need an ethics upon which their encounter with the Other is built. This ethics shall account for the radical difference of the Other. Justice in representations does not seem right if the Levinasian approach was followed. Rather, it appears that knowledge *itself* needs to be questioned if it is in the way of responsibility. Knowledge gathering cannot account for an ethical experience, regardless of whether it reflects justice of representation or not. Hence the focus shifts from an interest in "perfect knowledge" towards the actual interaction between individuals where infinite responsibility is put into effect. Responsibility ultimately makes the subject "aware of ethics as the possibility of doing otherwise than pursuing one's own interest" ((Aasland 2007), p. 226). At this point, I go back to the post-colonial argument that descriptions of cultures are the victim of power strategies. Levinasian ethics creates the possibility of overcoming the intention of following the own interests in the first place. As a consequence, one is able to experience the Other in an ethical way.

3.2.3   *The Levinasian Perspective on Business Ethics*

In this section I particularly refer to the work of Bevan and Corvellec as well as Jeanes and Muhr who reflected on business ethics from a Levinasian perspective ((Bevan, Corvellec 2007), (Jeanes, Muhr 2010)). The content of this section will be important for the deconstruction of cultural knowledge since it reveals an important point: knowledge has the power to replace individual responsibility and codified system represent a totality.

Some scholars have applied Levinasian ethics to analyze, criticize and investigate issues in today's business world. Academic writers have particularly focused on business ethics since its relevance has risen significantly in the business environment. Common strategies in the field aim to provide normative solutions that instruct employees how to act ethically. Hence it is assumed that one will act ethically if the right rules are at hand.

Jeanes and Muhr reflected on the topic from a Levinasian point of view and concluded that normative guidelines and codified systems remove any independence of thought. The reason is seen in a shift of responsibility from the individual towards written rules and norms (Jeanes, Muhr 2010). Further the individual aligns her/his behaviour according to what will be rewarded. Thus (s)he acts in terms of the right rules and not in light of her/his own responsibility. Rules and their inherent codified system take over the responsibility that is supposed to emanate from the individual. Loacker and Muhr further explained that codified ethics are a way of totalizing since they represent a closed system aiming to circumvent uncertainty and ambiguity (Loacker, Muhr 2009). However it is exactly in moments of uncertainty where Levinasian ethics call for the questioning of the self and pure responsibility towards the Other. Common approaches on the other hand shift responsibility towards an organizational level by setting up rules and norms.

At this point the question arises as to whether organisations in themselves are eligible to take over responsibility. Since ethics come into being during the encounter, the individual and not the organisation needs to act responsibly. Bevan and Corvellec indicated that a corporation does not represent a human being (Bevan, Corvellec 2007). It is not capable of opening itself to the otherness of the Other. Furthermore it does not experience any moral obligation towards other human beings. Ethics are therefore solely brought to existence through the individual. Thus rules and norms in themselves do not make organizations responsible (Jeanes, Muhr 2010). Levinasian ethics in addition points out that the fundamental otherness of the counterpart and unpredictability of the situation play an important role. These aspects make it difficult for individuals to align their behaviour to rules and norms.

Thus we can conclude at this point that any kind of prescribed rules for the encounter with the Other tend to take the individual's responsibility and shift it towards codified systems. This occurs in case one applies "business ethics" or cultural knowledge. This book claims that the latter constitutes cultures as codified systems just as rules and norms are represented in business ethics. Such an approach cannot account for Levinasian ethics.

To sum it up, Levinasian ethics introduce the reader to a different approach of experiencing the Other. It is a quest for an ethical relation to difference (Rhodes, Westwood 2007). Following Levinasian ethics leaves no choice but to question the primary role of knowledge that is so extensively supported by the discourse on cultural knowledge. The danger of denoting a primary role to (cultural) knowledge is the danger of reducing the

Other. These processes lead to totalities and merely serve the subordination to purposes (Ben-Ari, Strier 2010). It is the purpose of cultural knowledge to prepare individuals for the intercultural encounter by providing knowledge about cultures. Even though Levinasian ethics is very demanding, it serves well to provide a new perspective on cultural knowledge. In particular when it comes to ideas regarding interactions based on respect.

The next chapter presents the actual analysis of cultural knowledge. From a Levinasian perspective on the issue, I will reflect two aspects of Levinasian ethics on cultural knowledge: the shift of individual responsibility and the creation of totalities. The corresponding consequences for the individual who adopts cultural knowledge and the interest in interactions based on respect will be discussed.

4 Analysis of Cultural Knowledge

4.1 HISTORICAL BACKGROUND

The idea of gaining cultural knowledge is closely linked to the development of ICT. Both did not evolve until after the Second World War (the following review is based on (Rogers, Hart & Miike 2002)). The father of the practice was Edward T. Hall (1914 - 2009) who depicted the term "intercultural communication" in his book "The Silent Language" in 1959. However the first interests in intercultural communication, even though it was not termed as such then, occurred a few years earlier in the Foreign Service Institute of the United States. The institute was concerned about members of the diplomatic corps that were not effective abroad. The reason was not only seen in the lack of language skills but also in the missing knowledge about the culture of the country assigned to. The institute decided to provide language training which was conducted by native speakers in order to make sure the trainees learned the linguistic peculiarities of the language. Hall was part of the team of instructors and initially had the task to teach the corps about the macro-level of culture. However the participants complained about the trainings' content since a focus on the macro-level of cultures could not tell them how to communicate effectively. Hall learned about the importance not to simply provide information on a macro-level since it did not contain any information about particular characteristics of unfamiliar cultures and missed to teach strategies that help in new situations (Pusch 2004). The anthropological insights Hall used were too abstract. Consequently he changed his focus to a micro-level and to what is known today as "non-verbal communication". Hall was especially interested in the "out-of-awareness" level of communication and argued that one should pay attention to the subtle aspects of communication. His later book particularly emphasized proxemics (impact of space on communication) and chronemics (impact of time on communication).

The task of teaching American diplomats signified the foundation of the concept of cultural knowledge designed for ICT. It is important to note that the field was founded in the United States and has until today significantly been influenced by Western theories and scholars.

Cultural knowledge distinguishes itself from anthropological knowledge due to its focus on *inter*cultural communication. Hall was the first to develop such knowledge: he focused on (hidden factors of) communication between cultures instead of focusing on one particular culture in its anthropological terms. His cultural dimensions centre on the factors "context", "time" and "space". They are organized in binaries while cultures are understood to tend towards either of the groups ((Hall 1959), (Hall 1966)). As outlined above, the focus on aspects of the actual communication between cultures was regarded to be more concrete and useful due to its practical character. All this driven by a "need" to "function more effectively and sensitively with strange cultures during overseas assignments" ((Pusch 2004), p. 14).

Thus the main goal of cultural knowledge at that time was to increase effectiveness to accomplish the task or mission Americans were sent overseas for. Today the goal is the same, however the target has shifted from diplomatic corps to business people. Organizational interest in the field has grown due to an increase in failure/ineffectiveness of employees exposed to intercultural settings.

Since the 1960s several techniques for teaching intercultural communication have been developed. Intercultural workshops were conducted at American universities where international students were observed in interactions in order to investigate intercultural encounters. Corporations began to become interested in these trainings when they realized that Americans received negative attitudes abroad (Pusch 2004). In addition they became aware of the high cost of expatriate turnover in case of failure, which strengthened the interest to implement ICT. Europe developed its interest in the field slowly, starting in the Netherlands where the most popular, cited and applied research of cultural knowledge was conducted. In the next section the most important research in the field will be explained. Thereby I explain the content analyzed in this book.

4.2   THE CONTENT OF CULTURAL KNOWLEDGE

4.2.1   *Key Research and Influencing Factors*

This section introduces the main contributions to the field of cultural knowledge as it is used in ICT and outlines how these framed the concept of the field. It is important to note at this point that cultural knowledge can be divided into culture-specific versus culture-general knowledge: the former is concerned with a particular culture while the latter focuses on general knowledge regarding intercultural differences (Hammer 2000). Hammer indicated that a culture-specific approach aims to impart "communication competence" where rules of a specific culture are taught. The culture-general approach aims to teach those aspects of communication competence that are applicable across cultures. This book concerns itself with the latter since the RQ focuses on how cultural knowledge influences peoples' way of understanding by representing cultures in a certain way and whether it leads to encounters based on respect for cultural differences. Culture-specific knowledge on other hand teaches practical tips and tricks such as "dos and don'ts" in a specific country. It therefore "influences" peoples' practical actions, but does not necessarily aim at understanding in terms of the cultural values that influence one's way of communicating. The previous section explained the (historical) shift from anthropological knowledge towards general knowledge on communication differences. This was due to the need to understand what happened between people from different cultures when they communicate. This book investigates researches that were conducted for this purpose and therefore assesses the work of the three most important scholars in the field, namely Edward T. Hall, Geert Hofstede and Fons Trompenaars. Hall's work was introduced in the previous section. Thus this section turns to Hofstede and his four cultural dimensions.

Geert Hofstede developed four cultural dimensions in the 1980s. He later incorporated a fifth dimension, which was originally researched by a Canadian scholar. The dimensions distinguish cultures from each other by rating them according to their scores on each dimension (see (Hofstede 1980)). Hofstede's way of researching cultures was influenced by his definition of culture (see Introduction, section 1.3). Since he considered one culture to be a closed system adherent to a particular group, he displayed the "collective programming" by measuring it on the dimensions. In that way the groups could easily be compared to each other. By "group" Hofstede actually referred to nationalities; the results of his research portrayed the "collective programming" of 56 countries.

In the following I show an example of one of Hofstede's dimensions in detail in order to illustrate what he meant and referred to when describing a cultural dimension. The first dimension concerns the extent to which individualism or collectivism is reflected in a culture. He defines the binary dimension in the following:

> "Individualism on one side versus its opposite, collectivism, that is the degree to which individuals are inte-grated into groups. On the individualist side we find societies in which the ties between individuals are loose […]. On the collectivist side, we find societies in which people from birth onwards are integrated into strong, cohesive in-groups, often extended families […], which continue protecting them in exchange for unquestioning loyalty" (itim Culture and Management Consultancy 2009).

It is interesting to note that Hofstede understood individualism to be the opposite of collectivism. Hence, certain cultures are in opposition to other ones on account of this dimension. The other dimensions are concerned with Power Distance or the extent to which one expects power to be distributed unequally, Masculinity versus Femininity or the extent to which masculine/feminine values are distributed in a society and Uncertainty Avoidance or the extent to which there is tolerance to uncertainty and a need for structure and rules. The fifth dimension which was added later concerns Long-Term Orientation. While Long-Term Orientations stands for thrift and perseverance, Short-Term Orientation focuses on tradition and social obligations (Hofstede 1991). All five dimensions are conceptualized in binary oppositions. The book discusses the implications of this for those who acquire his knowledge.

Trompenaars based his work on Hall and Hofstede. He also developed cultural knowledge for the analysis of cultural differences (in communicative situations). Trompenaars introduced seven cultural dimensions that are also organized in binary oppositions. Examples are universalism versus particularism or the importance of rules versus connections. Another is achievement versus ascription or status ascribed through achievement or heritage (see (Trompenaars 1993)).

All three of them followed a descriptive approach to communication. As a consequence the knowledge helps to define cultural differences but leaves the application to the student.

However, they are all directed towards developing familiarity and minimizing situations where culture might create a source of irritation in terms of misunderstandings. Cultural knowledge is assumed to support individuals who face foreign cultures. It supposedly helps to prevent any source of irritation, which is associated with stress and potential failure (references will be given in the next section). Since the culturally foreign counterpart is not simply ruled over or dominated, but "understood" by cultural knowledge, the foundation for an interaction giving room to the counterpart's cultural values and habits is supposedly built.

There is one more aspect that needs to be pointed out in order to understand why cultural knowledge has been conceptualised the way it is: the significant influence of the corporate and business context. The participants of ICT are mainly students or employees who will be exposed to an intercultural environment at some point in the future. Hence cultural knowledge has been mainly used in a business context. Hall adjusted his work to the demands of American diplomats who asked for specific support in intercultural communication. The sponsors of cultural knowledge are mainly HR executives who initiate training for managers (Szkudlarek 2009). Both request tangible results and evident return on investment. In the case of cultural knowledge, they expect clear content, which is easy to understand and ready for immediate application. Scholars are therefore requested to deliver accordingly. Everything of low importance or minor contribution to the prevention of miscommunication and failure in intercultural encounters are excluded or ignored. The beneficial and constructive contribution of cultural knowledge is rather emphasized. In this way it is considered as "culturally defined business norms" ((Noerregard 2004), p. 210). Thus, cultural knowledge presents a guideline for intercultural encounters. Specificity is therefore needed and that is why Hall's, Hofstede's and Trompenaars' theories aimed to be very clear in their description of cultural differences. In so doing researchers become corporate consultants as they deliver knowledge, which is utilized for successful business interactions between people of differing cultural background.

The outlined aspect is of interest for the analysis since it points at political processes that might have an impact on the conceptualisation of cultural knowledge. As Alvesson and Deetz stated, we need to "encounter the political nature of management research" ((Alvesson, Deetz 1999), p. 7). If researchers acted as consultants for corporations, they might also incorporate the latter's conditions in their research. Mentioned aspects such as "return on investment" and clear content might have an influence. Both serve to close business deals and attain success all over the world. Thus there are interests of control;

without control success is at risk and failure becomes possible. These issues are important to keep in mind when it comes to the deconstruction of cultural knowledge.

4.2.2 Dominant Interpretation

An overall goal of ICT, which teaches cultural knowledge, is to assist people in developing positive and respectful relation to members of foreign cultures (Brislin, Yoshida 1994). As outlined in the introduction, understanding is equalized with respect. It is assumed that the achievement of a "vantage point" pays respect to another culture at the same time (Day 1998). At this point, I would already like to turn to the interviews to illustrate how this idea was reflected by the consultant. He stated the following:

> "If you can't understand you can't respect. If you can't respect you can't work with them. As simple as that" (I4).

He considered understanding as a foundation for respect. And respect is needed for successful work relationships. If cultural knowledge is regarded as the content for understanding it will also build the foundation for respect. These aspects represent the **dominant interpretation** of cultural knowledge.

The book now turns to the results of the interviews and questionnaires conducted in order to illustrate their points of view on respect. The following quotes are answers to the question regarding the extent to which the interviewees considered respect to be of importance in intercultural situations:

> "It is very important to have respect for the other culture otherwise you can not get along or understand them. Every culture (also your own culture) has special aspects that might look strange for others" (Q1).

> "Of course. Without being respectful you won't even get in touch with other cultures" (Q3).

> "Absolutely, because it makes people either feel comfortable or uncomfortable. If you want to have proper personal relationships, you always need to treat people respectfully. On top of that, I think it would be arrogant to assume that someone's own culture is superior (hence it would not be needed to treat other cultures with respect)" (Q4).

All three answers emphasized the importance of respect. I agree with them since intercultural communication constitutes encounters between human beings and everyone deserves to be treated with respect. As stated in the methodology the book does not aim to overrule the dominant interpretation by pursuing clotural reading. There is nevertheless something needed to support individuals in the encounter with people from other cultures. This book's interest is to destabilize the dominant interpretation's stability by pointing to limitations that ultimately undermine the idea of respect to the goal of providing understanding for the sake of control.

Before turning to the actual deconstruction, I reiterate the discussion of the terms "understanding" and "respect" that have already been initiated in the introduction of this book. The former stands for comprehension, while the latter reflects esteem and admiration for an issue or a person (Princeton University 2010). Demanding esteem and admiration is perhaps a bit too much asked for among cultures. And it is probably not what cultural knowledge aims to generate. It therefore appears that the term "respect" rather points to "tolerance", which is defined as permissiveness and the willingness to recognize the beliefs of others (Princeton University 2010). Freedom is granted to other practices or ideas and a liberal attitude gives room to their existence. This freedom granted is ultimately shown in acts of communication between human beings where one takes the other person seriously and treats her/him with sincerity. Based on these thoughts cultural knowledge is expected to give a clear and neutral picture of cultural differences that helps to tolerate differences on the basis of equal grounds.

With these issues in mind an analysis of cultural knowledge is made. The book aims to find evidence of the extent to which cultural knowledge supports or prevents the development of respect for other cultures. Even though the study understands respect in terms of tolerance, the term "respect" will be adopted since it was used in the introduction and is mentioned several times by scholars and interviewees. The intention to deconstruct the concept of cultural knowledge and point at blind spots of the same, required to structure the analysis accordingly.

4.3 DECONSTRUCTING CULTURAL KNOWLEDGE

4.3.1 The Post-colonial Perspective on Cultural Knowledge

4.3.1.1 The Constitution of Cultural Differences as a Threat

This section elaborates how cultural knowledge is constituted as an aid to deal with the "threat" of cultural differences and how this ultimately hinders interactions based on respect.

The argument is inspired by PCT which claimed that the West structures the world on the scale of modernization and considers countries with a lack in modernization as being in opposition to Western countries. Attributes such as wild and undeveloped are ascribed to the former. Hence from a Western perspective, it becomes necessary to find a way to deal with them in order to secure Western structures of modernization. Today these structures are associated with capitalism. Strategies to deal with these cultures find their justification in considering the latter as being a threat to modernization, thus a threat to capitalism. If this is true, political interests to maintain the status quo lead to these strategies. Political interests can gain a significant dominance, in particular, if they are related to power strategies. The argument that other cultures present a threat to Western ways of modernization, capitalism and therefore doing business could connect the outlined arguments with cultural knowledge.

In order to analyze how this argument is reflected by cultural knowledge I look at the discourse on cultural knowledge and give voice to statements of scholars in the field. Here it is in particular of interest how scholars define the goal of cultural knowledge, meaning what it aims to achieve. The first quote is cited from Hofstede's homepage. The second statement is quoted from an article that discussed developments in the area of intercultural communication. The third statement was quoted from a chapter in a handbook on intercultural competence.

Geert Hofstede's website gives an overview to his work and states clearly what his research aims to accomplish:

> "Geert Hofstede's research gives us insights into other cultures so that we can be more effective when interacting with people in other countries. If understood and applied properly, this information should reduce your level of frustration, anxiety, and concern. But most important, Geert Hofstede will give you the 'edge of

understanding', which translates to more successful results" (itim Culture and Management Consultancy 2009).

Cultural knowledge such as Hofstede's cultural dimensions has extensively been used in ICT. Since they are closely related and aim at the same direction, some statements regarding the purpose of ICT are cited in the following:

> ICT „eliminat[e] misunderstandings and conflicts in international personnel exchange schemes and enhanc[e] the benefits arising from international cooperation" ((Engelbert 2004), p. 195).

Jaeger (1995), referring to Dadder, stated the following:

> "The purpose of these courses is not primarily the professional preparation; they rather focus on preparing the participants for cultural phenomena and problems, which may arise in interaction with foreign cultures" (Dadder (1987) in (Jaeger 1995), p. 35, translation by the author).

Cultural knowledge and ICT aim to prepare individuals in order to prevent emotional stress, misunderstandings, conflicts and problems that might arise in situations with members of foreign cultures. This shall ultimately lead to "more successful results" and "benefits". The intercultural encounter is therefore perceived as a situation filled with problems if not guarded against determinately. Success becomes possible if the problems are dealt with.

Just as the consultant interviewed stated:

> We are "giving them basic tools for handling cultural differences and bridging a cultural gap and solving communication problems and giving them a different mindset about how to work with people who are basically not like yourself" (I4).

Cultural knowledge serves as a mean to "bridge the cultural gap". It is understood as a tool to deal with the challenges cultural differences are assumed to implicate.

All these quotes state that there is a danger of conflict, misunderstanding, mistakes and so forth if one is not able to deal with cultural differences. Hence cultural differences are perceived as threats for the success of an interaction. The solution to these threats is seen in the management of the situation. Cultural knowledge is considered as the prerequisite in order to understand what one is supposed to manage. Without this knowledge mistakes or miscommunication can lead to failed conversations or more importantly in the business world, the collapse of a business deal.

The statements additionally show how cultural knowledge is based on an interest in control. By gaining knowledge about how the culturally other person is like one assumes to be able to deal with differences. (S)he can manage them in order to make sure that neither control is lost nor conflicts or misunderstandings are given room to arise. Gaining cultural knowledge is therefore significantly influenced by an idea of control.

I herewith illustrate how those who adopted cultural knowledge have picked up the idea of seeing cultural differences as a threat. When some of the interviewees were asked how and why they thought that cultural knowledge is of help in intercultural encounters, they gave the following answers:

> "Without any pre-knowledge about Arabic culture, I would have definitely needed something. Cause otherwise it's too risky to go down there. I would do too many stupid mistakes" (I1).

> "It helps avoiding unnecessary conflicts and it also helps in situations once a conflict has occurred. It is easier to understand the other person and hence easier to deal with the conflict in a productive manor" (Q4).

> "The acquired knowledge has helped me to understand foreign clients' behaviour in a better way. The knowledge is relevant to understand other people's behaviour and habits better in order to avoid miscommunication, work together and reach a common goal" (Q5).

Hence cultural knowledge shall help to support productivity and is therefore of high relevance in international business settings. It becomes an important means in business interactions and transactions. They in turn represent an important part of capitalism. Both quotes reflect the earlier-mentioned argument: cultural differences can turn into a threat if not known and/or dealt with. Here they mainly referred to the threat of conflicts, miscommunication and failure of productivity. Therefore there appears a connection between the purpose of cultural knowledge and Western capitalist (business) interests since the former serves as a means to maintain the latter.

The study's concern in this regard points at the consequences for those who acquire cultural knowledge: the idea of control or management shifts the focus to differences which are considered as the cause of a threat that needs to be dealt with. Those who participate in lectures or trainings are told that cultural differences lead to conflict and miscommunication if not understand in the right way. Thus they are almost forced to learn cultural knowledge out of the necessity to prevent any kind of failure in business situations. The point here is that the constitution of cultural differences as a threat rather leads to the enhancement than reduction of distance and fear of potential problems. How shall one be capable to openly encounter members of other cultures if (s)he rather fears miscommunication, conflict and failure and aims to do anything to prevent it? The negative perception of cultural differences makes the individual stick to the adopted cultural knowledge in fear of not being able to control the situation. In that way knowledge is given more importance than an open unprejudiced encounter. It is prior to openness towards the specificity of the intercultural situation and, more importantly, the individuality of the counterpart.

Cultural knowledge or those who formulate its purpose missed to emphasize positive aspects that may arise out of intercultural encounters. Examples are exchange and mutual learning. Instead the focus is placed on negative aspects cultural differences might lead to. At the end of the day, these are probably both relevant. However focusing only on threats and therefore influencing those who take on cultural knowledge in their perception of cultural differences does not lead to an encounter based on respect. If those who study cultural knowledge are not made aware of potential negative *and* positive outcomes, the intercultural interaction is merely perceived as a situation that creates stress and needs to be managed in order to prevent failure. Of course, there might be miscommunication, but why can it not be understood as a process of enrichment? Turning back to PCT and the argument that Western interests strive to maintain power relationships it seems that the aspect of control prevents any openness to new insights. If openness prevails there is a potential risk of unforeseen and contra-productive (in a capitalist sense) situations. This is not acceptable from a business perspective since business transactions and tasks need to be done.

To what extent unforeseen situations are not welcomed in a business transaction is illustrated by one of the interviewees. The respondent was asked to explain her reaction in situations where she experienced a cultural difference or miscommunication she did not know about or did not expect:

"Sometimes we need some results. Because what we do is we try to be task oriented, we try to focus on the task at hand. And then getting that task solved. Now if I don't get through with the communication with the product manager to whom I usually speak, then I need to go a step up. Cause usually I don't have much time to wait for information or…" (here she changed to another topic) (I2).

Her main goal was to get the task done. And if she got stuck due to miscommunication or else, she "went one step up" to the manager whom she hoped can prevent the task from failure due to his positional power. She further justified her approach by submitting to time pressure. However the openness to the culturally foreign person ends where communication fails and time pressure rises. And in order to protect the entire task from failure, she asked her manager to proceed. If he cannot get through with the (same) communication either he has at least the power to line up the task's success. Power in this case is expected to overrule cultural difference. If openness and understanding face limits, positional power is used to make things work. The example shows that the pressure to get a task done advances the negative perception of miscommunication. Hence the business world and its conditions are perhaps the source of the outlined negative connotation. The outlined purpose of cultural knowledge however strengthens these tendencies. Instead of putting miscommunication into perspective, cultural knowledge becomes an agent of the Western business world and intensifies the perception that cultural differences represent a threat.

This section started off with PCT's argument pointing out that power and control interests are part of Western knowledge creation. The constitution of cultural differences as a threat was illustrated by stating quotes from scholars and interviewees regarding the overall goal of cultural knowledge. The next section deals with the issue on the contents of cultural knowledge.

4.3.1.2 Binary Oppositions and Underlying Interpretations

This section outlines the PCT argument that cultural representations are rather a product of Western rationality than a reflection of reality. It is analyzed how this argument is reflected by cultural knowledge and how the organisation of cultural differences in binary oppositions contributes to a certain perception of cultures. Further results of the interviews and questionnaires illustrate how those who adopt cultural knowledge make sense of difference.

PCT takes the view that power interests significantly influence representations of cultures. Thereby certain representations are favoured over others (Kwek 2003). The goal to maintain order and control requires that representations are easily understood and give a clear (usable) picture of reality. Cultures are therefore organized in clearly distinguishable categories. Said determinately criticized the Western way of representing others and considered the process to be a cultural production. He stated that representations of cultures are "produced" by reference to the West in opposition to a reflection of reality (Said 1978). Further cultural knowledge is one-sided. The voice of those represented here is not given any room since representations solely contain a Western voice. Including the voice of the described culture could lead to an increase in the representations' reliability. This idea has apparently not been considered from scholars of cultural knowledge though. If cultural knowledge is one-sided and influenced by political strategies, reliability becomes questionable since we do not know whether they depict reality in a "true" way.

Hofstede and his colleagues describe cultures in "cultural dimensions". If a culture accounts for a certain cultural dimensions, one can only understand what it signifies if it is reflected in one's own culture. Hence there is a "starting point" needed that each category relates to. In case of cultural knowledge the starting point is given by a Western understanding of reality. Every culture is therefore "measured" in terms of what Western rationality assumes to be an important and normal (!) issue of reality. Hofstede's cultural dimensions state for example the following: Singaporeans and Indonesians are considered to have a high acceptance of unequally distributed power and Peruvians as well as Thai are described as showing very low individualism, meaning the society is collectivist (itim Culture and Management Consultancy 2009). We need to ask for the reference to which these countries are considered high in power distance and low in individualism. The reference is a Western perception of reality.

Hall and Trompenaars organized their dimensions in a similar way. Hall did not conduct systematic research that rates countries on cultural dimensions. However his dimensions are also conceptualized in binary oppositions. He for example ascribes cultures that reflect a tendency for High Context to communicate in simple messages with deep meaning, however feelings undergo strict self-control. Low Context cultures on the other hand communicate in a more explicit but less personal way (Hall 1976). While Hall himself did not rate any countries or cultures, other scholars conducted research in that matter. As a result, Asian countries such as China, Korea and Japan were attributed to High Context cultures while Switzerland, United States and the Scandinavian countries are seen to reflect

Low Context cultures ((Kim, Pan & Park 1998), (Onkvisit, Shaw 1993)). Trompenaars described among other dimensions the way cultures look at time. Sequential Time Orientation makes people do one thing at a time while Synchronic Time Orientation inspires to do several things at the same time (Trompenaars 1993). Trompenaars added in graphs to his description of the dimensions that showed ratings of several countries. Here European and American countries are seen to reflect Sequential Time Orientation while South American and Middle Eastern countries are considered to reflect Synchronic Time Orientation.

This book does not intend to judge the correctness of these statements. What is of interest here is the organisation of cultures in binary oppositions. As mentioned above, we need to ask for the reference to which countries/cultures are described to be high or low in context or reflect sequential or synchronic orientation towards time. Each culture appears to reflect more or less issues, which are considered significant in Western terms. Thus it either reflects Western terms or it does not. The consequence is a binary distinction between Western and Non-Western cultures. Furthermore they constitute comparisons of black versus white and ultimately good versus bad. In order to clarify this argument I turn to Kim's reflection on Hofstede's cultural dimensions.

Kim concluded in her critical reflection on Hofstede's contribution to cultural knowledge that the binary conception of cultural dimensions contains subliminal interpretations. These interpretations may in turn influence the perception of (Western) students of cultural knowledge (Kim 2007). She discussed particularly the example of "individualism vs. collectivism" (Hofstede's definition of this cultural dimension was cited in section 4.2). Kim observed the dichotomy to appear mutually exclusive to a Western eye since the individual and the group are presumed to be in opposition to each other. For example, limiting an individual's potential by ascribing her/him to either of the binary oppositions does not bear up if one has a multicultural background. Binary categories tend to gloss over nuances and subtle differences. They therefore represent a simplified picture of reality. Further she pointed to consequences: black-and-white categories do not only limit understanding, they also lead to good versus bad comparisons. And what one refers to as good or bad is deeply rooted in an understanding of reality. In the case of "individualism vs. collectivism" the former is favoured over the latter in Western environments. Why? Kim saw the cause in the appreciation of self-containment and separation of the individual *a priori* that demand to be critical about the collective. She refers to Klein who agued that relationality is termed to threaten the "right" of the realization of the self (Klein 1995).

Loosing or being derogated in one's realization of the self becomes equivalent to loosing self-value. Whether the tendency to rate individualism as good and collectivism as bad is justified shall not be the interest of this book. It is rather of interest to highlight the bias of binary categories and point at the subsequent consequence of a particular interpretation of reality and judgement of good and bad.

In order to illustrate how individuals who learn cultural knowledge relate to binary oppositions when making sense of cultural differences, the interviewees were asked about the biggest cultural differences they had experienced. The following presents some of the responses to the question:

> "I think that time management differs a lot across cultures. In some cultures people do different things at the same time, in others they do one thing after the other. And coming to the point/timetable of a meeting differs: in some cultures people talk a lot before they get to the point. In Italy, I experienced for example that meetings do not really have a timetable. People meet, chat for a while and then start working. In my country we do not waste time by chatting at the beginning for a long time" (Q1).

Another one said:

> "There are some basic rules [...] I learnt in my intercultural training at the business school. It is that you need to define whether a culture is individualist or collectivist. Because that has a fundamental effect on how people react [....]. Cause the individualist culture will *always* be able to question [...]. Whereas a collectivist culture would *never* do that."

Later she also stated an example (referring to the last sentence of the previous quote):

> "The Taiwanese employees don't make any decisions. And if they are told: 'Go do that', they will do it no matter what and if it makes a house burn down, they don't care, because their boss told them. [...] There is no reflection, it's not a cultural way you are asked to reflect upon your orders, you are asked to perform and to just go and do it.
>
> And when that meets a Danish culture or a Northern European culture where you are not asked to go and do it if it's stupid; think – for bloody sake! (laughter) Think about what you are asked to do and if you can provide an even better solution so that the result is equal or better then you are expected to come up with a suggestion. It's very rare that we in this country go and say: 'you have to perform a certain task in a very specific way' - unless it is required by law" (I2).

These statements reflect some of the dimensions cultural knowledge teaches about. The first quote mentions Trompenaars' dimension of "sequential versus synchronic" time management. The second quote clearly states Hofstede's dimension on individualist versus collectivist. The third quote exemplifies how Hofstede's dimension is experienced in practice. Here I would like to point at the way the interviewees made sense of difference by applying cultural dimensions. By referring to one's own culture subconsciously or consciously, one defines a "standard" of how things work due to experience. These (Western) standards are reflected in the cultural dimensions, mainly as one extreme on the scale of the dimension. The behaviour of foreign cultures is rated in relation to one's own. Here cultural dimensions help to find words for these differences. The point is that one usually perceives the "standard", thus one's own way of doing things, as the good way. Other ways are consequently considered to be in opposition to the good way. The quotes show a negative perception of the difference between cultures: chatting at the beginning of a meeting is considered "a waste of time". Further the negative perception of the Taiwanese culture where people rather execute orders than pursue reflection is called upon the interviewee by stating: "think – for bloody sake". Hence members of the Taiwanese culture are perceived to not think on their own terms. This is considered a consequence of collectivism as the interviewee stated. These examples are a consequence of the ethnocentric nature of cultural dimensions. Hofstede, Hall and Trompenaars have been criticized to impose ethnocentrism upon their research (see for example (Fougere, Moulettes 2007), (Walle 1990)). Ethnocentrism is defined to constitute the "belief in the superiority of one's own ethnic group" (Princeton University 2010).

The interest of this book is to point out what ethnocentric approaches describing cultural differences miss to include. They do not account for various perspectives on reality. In this way they do not create understanding in terms of *why* certain cultures might do things in a particular way. The example above exemplifies this argument: The interviewee's perception does not include the aspect that Asian cultures long for harmony and their focus on relationships make them withhold their own opinion. The importance of harmonious relationships is given more weight here since individual opinions are regarded as a lack of group membership (Xue 2003). Hence Asian cultures tend to give high value to group membership. Turning back to the example of the interviewee it becomes obvious that there is a certain understanding (comprehension) that Taiwanese people might react the way they do. But it is limited to the facts of the experience and the knowledge taught in ICT. There is no *real* understanding *why* the Taiwanese culture acts the way they do. More importantly there is no reflection that their way of handling things might be reputable as well. Since the interviewee is "stuck" in her own perception of reality she is limited in her respectful attitude towards the Taiwanese culture. Of course, these examples might be exceptions. However the argument here is that the interviewee's tendency to have a negative perspective on cultural differences is strengthened rather than prevented by cultural knowledge as it has been conceptualized so far. Cultural knowledge does not support (Western) individuals to see the world from different angles. Nor does it create understanding in terms of tolerance/respect for how other cultures might do things differently. It only describes cultural representations from a Western point of view. If those who take on this knowledge are not aware of its one-sidedness they tend to perceive cultural differences in a negative way. To put it in Blasco's words: information substitutes understanding (Blasco 2004). There is information about how the other culture "works", but there is no understanding, let alone tolerance or respect, if one does not comprehend why other ways of doing things occur.

It is quite likely that Hofstede and his colleagues did not intend to deliberately attach subliminal interpretations to their work and were merely interested in expanding knowledge about intercultural difference. The problem here is that they assumed neutrality in their research which is not the case. The example of cultural knowledge shows how any author is the victim of her/his cultural subjective position (Rhodes, Westwood 2007). Cultural background, values and an understanding of right and wrong significantly influence the author's perception of reality. In turn the way of writing and knowledge creation are affected. The author gains authority by giving voice while other voices are silenced at the same time (Calás, Smircich 1999). Hence the writing is limited to a certain perspective and the author's background impairs the constitution of the objects (s)he studies. The consequence is a colonization of thought due to the control of discourse where the functionalist paradigm "imposes the reality they seek to describe" ((Kwek 2003), p. 122). In terms of cultural knowledge the "collision" of an interest to understand cultures with a biased representation of the same is therefore seen. Is the only way out of the dilemma to give up on the idea of representation, assuming that justice of representation – in terms of a neutral way of knowledge gathering – is impossible? Alvesson suggests "reflexive pragmatism", which "calls for epistemological awareness rather than philosophical rigor" ((Alvesson 2003), p. 25). We need to be aware of the possibility of multiple perspectives on reality and understand that one way of framing might veil another one. Cultural knowledge explains cultural differences, but it misses to explain why there are certain differences. Thus it creates perceptions in those who adopt the knowledge since they have no choice but to compare the other way of doing things to their own. Ultimately negative perceptions are likely to occur.

Cultural knowledge as introduced by Hall, Hofstede and Trompenaars is assumed to be neutral. However it is the product of a Western perception of reality. Cultural knowledge is therefore easily understandable to people from a Western background and comprehension takes place. However does cultural knowledge also build the foundation for tolerance, let alone respect? The interviewees' statements as well as the discussion revealed that cultural knowledge contains subliminal interpretations. This is due to the conception of cultural differences as binary oppositions from a Western perspective. Subliminal interpretations have the potential to shape the cultural knowledge student's perception of other cultures. The quotes from the interviews illustrated how cultural differences may be perceived in a negative way. Cultural knowledge contributes to this limitation by "compromising" in the representation. Tolerance on the grounds of a liberal understanding and equal rights is therefore not confirmed by the argument of this section.

Turning back to PCT, Ashcroft et al.'s argument needs some attention. They stated that cultural representations as they are currently used entail binary oppositions leading to the establishment of dominance (Ashcroft, Griffiths & Tiffin 1998). It was indicated in the previous section that cultural knowledge serves the interest to maintain power interests of capitalism. Spivak described cultural representations as "thick with context" where bodies of knowledge obscure the powerful messages about cultures (Spivak 1993a). In this way they shape people's concept of cultural identities (Jack, Lorbiecki 2003). Furthermore they contribute to the establishment of neo-colonial control where Western cultures are considered superior to others (Prasad 2003). We see a similar process outlined in this section: binary oppositions inherent in cultural knowledge potentially influence those who have learned about it in their perception of cultures. PCT-scholars see in this process a contribution to neo-colonial power, meaning the power interests of capitalist societies. This section might have supported their argument to a certain extent since a negative perception towards other ways of doing things does not aid support of the same. Due to their negative perception of other cultures people stay with the well-known and positively perceived state of the art. Thus they indirectly support capitalism. Based on the arguments of this section I come to the conclusion that representations of cultures as they are given in cultural knowledge are limited in their explanation *why* cultures behave the way they do. Those who adopt cultural knowledge are therefore "stuck" in their own perception of reality; this leads to good versus bad comparisons. Hence one may be hampered to realize interaction based on respect.

In terms of understanding and respect, this section leads to the following conclusion: Understanding is accomplished by cultural knowledge to the extent that it reflects Western perceptions of reality. Non-Western cultures are only understood in Western terms. Cultural knowledge is therefore biased. As a consequence those who acquire the knowledge are not given the opportunity to *really* understand other cultures since they are foreclosed the real meaning behind unfamiliar values. By real I refer to an accurate representation that explains why people do things in a particular way. Thus I do not see a respectful way of representing cultures. Explanations and various perspectives are missing to accomplish comprehension that ultimately leads to respect. Furthermore the opportunity to tolerate let alone respect the difference of culturally others to one's own is not facilitated since binary dimensions lead to good versus bad comparisons if the mentioned explanations are not given. To conclude, understanding in a biased way is given more importance than respectful representations or respect for cultural differences.

4.3.1.3 Homogenization and Simplification

This section demonstrates how cultural knowledge constitutes cultures in homogenized and simplified dimensions. The results of interviews illustrate how students of cultural knowledge have adopted this perspective on cultures. After which a discussion follows on how the knowledge on cultures is a victim of the predominant interest to control and what this implies for the individual who adopts cultural knowledge and is exposed to intercultural encounters.

Another aspect PCT criticized is directed at homogenizations and simplification that prevail in cultural representations. Kwek states that such processes serve the interest to more easily engage knowledge about "the objects of the world" (Kwek 2003). If knowledge is clearly structured in understandable parts it can more easily be applied as a mean to achieve certain ends. PCT considered these processes as a homogenization and simplification of reality and argued that they cannot account for the complex nature of cultures. Members of other cultures are considered as objects that can easily be understood and therefore handled. Jack and Westwood saw this as a clear advantage for the business world and stated that cultures are described in a way that made them understandable in order to support business and trade practices and therefore secure economic advantages

(Jack, Westwood 2006). If there is an interest to establish and maintain control, clear guidelines are needed that guide the way. Here I return to cultural knowledge in order to investigate the manner in which homogenization and simplification are reflected. Quotes from the interviews later illustrate the points made that are discussed in terms of the corresponding consequences.

It was earlier mentioned that Hofstede equalizes one culture with one national state in his research. He generated a list on numerous cultures/nationalities and their scores on the cultural dimensions. However there was no attention paid to sub-cultures or individual differences that might appear within a nationality. Thus homogenization takes place since human beings are ascribed by nationality to certain cultural dimensions. Further simplification occurred since factors such as context, organizational as well as social relationships were excluded from the picture (Bjerregaard, Lauring & Klitmøller 2009). Simplification also takes place in terms of fixation since any potential changes or deviances are excluded from the picture. If cultural knowledge paid attention to individual differences, subcultures and other influencing factors, it could get "out of hand" and become a useless tool in the struggle for control. Boundaries would be threatened and knowledge could not fit into neat categories anymore (Jack, Lorbiecki 2003). Hence manipulation of cultural knowledge and the disregard of additional factors are according to PCT the result of a clear priority on control and power. PCT claims that clear structures are needed to establish control. Hence "difficult or intransigent material [is manipulated] into a form that facilitates control" ((Cooper 1992), p. 255).

The interviewees were asked to exemplify how cultural knowledge has helped them. Some of the answers are as follows:

"When I suggested something to Chinese people, they were smiling the whole time and if they had disagreed I would have been very surprised. As I know that it is part of/ polite in the Chinese culture to smile I know how to deal with this" (Q1).

"The knowledge about indirect communication helped me to make an effort to communicate with the Portuguese / and also discuss these topics with peers" (Q2).

"I got involved in a public-private-partnership project with Japan. Japanese people stay their entire life with the company they've once started to work for. Being aware of this cultural characteristic has helped me to better respond to the client" (Q5).

These quotes illustrate Hofstede's concept of culture where one nationality represents one culture. The interviewees regard all the members of a certain nationality to be unitary in the cultural habits and values: Chinese smile and do not disagree, Portuguese communicate indirectly and Japanese stay with one company their entire life. Each person is by nationality ascribed to certain values. Cultural knowledge frames cultures in cohesive, closed groups. As a consequence the world becomes a better-organized place and students of cultural knowledge easily comprehend the differences between supposedly unitary cultural groups, namely nationalities. The same argument accounts for Trompenaars who ascribed nationalities to his dimensions accordingly. Hall on the other hand did not focus on particular countries. However his research has still undergone simplification and fixation. Cultural knowledge is therefore the result of homogenization, simplification and furthermore fixation and limited regarding an idea of respectful representations.

The main concern in this regard points out that cultural knowledge is limited to serve as a basis for the understanding (comprehension) of cultural difference. Since its preciseness ends with the "border" of national cultures or a few aspects, it excludes additional important factors. If those who study cultural knowledge are not aware of these limitations they are likely to gloss over nuances. Further they cannot account for the specificity of the situation. However there might be exceptions to the rule and individuals do not reflect the dimension their nationality is ascribed to. ·The individual who adheres to simplified and homogenized knowledge could easily miss subtleties or exceptions.

This is reminiscent of Bhabha's argument on the ineffectiveness of stereotypes. Rhodes and Westwood endorsed his argument and indicated that the ineffectiveness of stereotypes becomes obvious as soon as they are not fulfilled in the interaction (Rhodes, Westwood 2007). Recognizing the ineffectiveness requires that one is sensitive to depict exceptions from the rule. And cultural knowledge does not seem to make its students aware of exceptions. Thus if those who acquire cultural knowledge are either not sensitive towards or made aware of exceptions, they probably tend to miss nuances and peculiarities.

Further, what does the argument pointing at the acceptance of homogenization and simplification for the sake of control imply for interactions based on respect? If cultural knowledge is the victim of the predominant interest to control, the human factor has to take a back seat in the intercultural encounter. Open, honest and sincere encounters between human beings are not given the priority. Of course, this might also depend highly on the individual or the situation. However if students of cultural knowledge are not aware of the homogenized and simplified representation of (national) cultures, understanding in terms of the counterpart's personality as well as contextual factors is compromised. Ultimately openness towards differences and therefore tolerance undergoes impairment.

4.3.1.4 Synthesis of the Post-colonial Perspective

The previous sections have outlined the trajectory of the consequences of cultural knowledge in its current constitution. Consequences were particularly highlighted for interactions based on respect or rather tolerance that gives room to the counterpart's (cultural) specificity and ascribes equal rights to their existence. It was described how cultural knowledge is presented as a tool to avoid miscommunication, which might arise if one is not aware of cultural differences. However miscommunication, conflicts and so on are rendered as negative aspects, therefore, a threat. And more importantly there is no intention to render intercultural communication as a process of mutual learning and enrichment. Cultural differences appear as the source of these threats. I therefore claim that it is very challenging for the individual to maintain a positive perspective on cultural differences if (business) communication is endangered and meant to fail. Hence cultural knowledge and its respective goal become a process aimed at control instead of openness and tolerance, let alone respect.

The book further outlined how cultural knowledge is organised in binary oppositions. Analysis showed how these oppositions are products of a Western mindset and contain underlying interpretation. As a consequence students of cultural knowledge tend to perceive cultural differences in extremes such as good versus bad particularly if they are not made aware of the missing neutrality and one-sidedness of cultural knowledge. Yet again, tolerance is challenged by a negative perception of differences.

In the previous and last section of the actual analysis the homogenization, simplification and fixation of cultures as they are represented in cultural knowledge was discussed. Hofstede particularly accounted for homogenization since he equalizes culture with nationality. Simplification however is attributed to the cultural knowledge based on the research of all three scholars. Their cultural dimensions only cover parts of the numerous influences on intercultural encounters. They might have given a "clear" picture in terms of comprehensibility since the world is clearly structured and the knowledge easily understandable. However the cost are homogenization and simplification. If the student of cultural knowledge is not made aware of these limitations, (s)he is likely to miss personal characteristics, context and exceptions from the rule and is therefore hampered to account for the specificity of the situation. Again cultural knowledge seems to mainly represent a tool for the maintenance of control. If this is the case, major concerns on the humanity of intercultural encounters between human beings were raised.

The arguments of the three sections led to the conclusion that cultural knowledge is a victim of control interests. In this regard it offers understanding (comprehension), even though limited, of cultural differences in order to enable the individual to prevent the intercultural encounter to get out of hand. Since cultural knowledge has been conceptualized from a Western perspective, it has a tendency to shed Western ways of doing things in a positive light. Following PCT the power interests, namely the interest to maintain capitalism, predominates. The analysis so far leads to a similar conclusion: the intention of control has become very clear. And even though there is an interest to understand cultures in their specificity, room is only given to the extent that it does not threaten control. And in turn it does not threaten their own, Western, way of doing business. Thus cultural knowledge provides understanding to a certain extent. However if students are not made aware of limitations they could be hindered in the development of tolerance.

In my search for support regarding intercultural encounter based on respect, cultural knowledge appears to be limited. Understanding to serve control seems to take priority over respectful representations. Hence the individual who adheres to cultural knowledge is limited to develop respect for cultural differences.

The next sections focus on Levinasian ethics. The main ideas of his philosophy were presented in the literature review. I reflect once more on cultural knowledge in order to understand how its current conceptualisation hampers the means towards encounters based on respect from a Levinasian perspective.

4.3.2 *The Levinasian Perspective on Cultural Knowledge*

4.3.2.1 Replacing Individual Responsibility with Knowledge

Levinas understood every encounter between human beings as an ethical institution and claimed that infinite responsibility should be at the centre of each relationship. Ethics is understood as "first philosophy" and therefore prior to ontology. Levinas ascribes enormous importance to responsibility and questions knowledge in general if it hinders the former in any way. His approach is based on two main points of critique: the replacement of individual responsibility through knowledge and the constitution of knowledge as a totality. Neither accounts for the incomprehensiveness of the Other nor the specificity of a situation. This section focuses on the first point of critique.

Levinas encourages infinite responsibility by allowing the Other to interrupt the self, the ego, the knowing subject that usually reduce otherness to the same (Critchley 1999). Otherness appears on the other hand if one lets interruption and disconnection happen and refrains from translation and calculation (Muhr 2008a). The encounter with the Other is therefore according to Levinas beyond being and ontology. Otherness cannot be accommodated with any theories. Rather it is located in a point of "exteriority" and beyond any representational thinking (Critchley 1999). Accepting these Levinasian conditions enables access to otherness. Deviance and new insights are given room if one remains open. And ultimately "true" significance, thus, understanding of the "real" reality is obtained. To say it in Levinas terms: re-sponsibility towards the otherness of the Other becomes possible.

As far as cultural knowledge is concerned, Levinas directs the attention to the replacement of individual responsibility through knowledge. Here the individual is freed from his own responsibility since the behaviour is guided by normative categories. The example of business ethics (see section 3.2.3) has already demonstrated the process of a shift in responsibility. Ethical norms provide a sense of security since the individual can adjust his behaviour according to the norms. Further they relieve the individual of responsibility by removing any independence of thought (Jeanes, Muhr 2010).

To see how this is reflected in cultural knowledge, the results obtained from scholars who discussed the "outcome" of knowledge on cultural differences when applied in the right way are presented. The quotes are excerpts from handbooks on intercultural competence. As Hammer explained in a chapter on "Intercultural Communication Competence":

> „Behaviour is appropriate when it meets contextual and relational standards or expectations and effective when it is functional in achieving desirable ends or goals or satisfying interactants' needs." ((Hammer 2000), p. 248)

He also explained the concept of "cultural competence", which is measured to the extent to which the individual has learned culture-specific rules of communication. One is encouraged to relate to "contextual and relational standards" and attain cultural competence. In so doing "appropriate behaviour" occurs in order to satisfy needs. The "standards" are framed in cultural knowledge since it claims to teach about "standards" in a foreign culture. Hammer's statement further implies that meeting the standards becomes a mean to serve the achievement of certain ends. In other words: ends cannot be achieved if one does not adjust her/his behaviour to "standards". The focal point in the above is control.

As Jaeger stated in a chapter on "Teaching Culture – State of the Art":
> "Information concerning the foreign culture to the future intercultural actor is supposed to result into something qualitative different form cognitively acquired information, namely skilfully performed action in an intercultural setting" ((Jaeger 1995), p. 33)

"Skilfully performed action" is achieved as soon as one has gathered "information" and adjusted behaviour according to the latter. The individual is therefore well advised to turn to "information", thus cultural knowledge. Again "information" becomes a mean to an end. Knowledge can be converted to a manual directing the interaction with members of a foreign culture.

The consequence is the following: adhering to knowledge is given more importance than an open way to encounter the other person. Levinas stated that knowledge prevents openness to re-spond to the Other. He encouraged the individual to be responsive depending on what the Other offers, says or how (s)he acts. To his mind one is rather supposed to decide in the situation itself how to react instead of letting knowledge lead the way.

Responsibility according to Levinas is not achieved by acquiring rational models in order to achieve a certain end. To his understanding responsibility is prior to rationality and refrains from being responsible for the sake of anything. This is because we are human beings and the encounter with the Other demands infinite responsibility (Aasland 2007). From a Levinasian perspective and in terms of what was argued above, cultural knowledge does not leave any space for an ethical experience of the Other marked by openness, generosity and respect for otherness. In order to illustrate Levinas' argument and point out the consequence, examples from the interviewees are presented in the following:
> "When you deal with Germans, be precise! Don't give them any story; don't talk too

much […]. Give them the truth and then discuss with them what is the proper cause of action."

And later added:

"Be extremely honest. They hate it if you are not honest with them" (I2).

Whenever she meets a person with German background she knows what to do since her knowledge directs the assumed proper behaviour. According to Levinas any kind of knowledge forecloses openness towards the Other. In the case of the example, I can reflect on the statement from the Other's point of view since my background is a German one. The interviewee was not aware of my German background at the time being. Thus I experienced the following: even though the statements might be true to a certain extent, further help to avoid "miscommunication" and decrease uncertainty on the interviewee's side I was surprised of the way I was pigeonholed. To say it in Levinasian terms: I felt as if I was made into an identity and robbed of my individuality. The interviewee's knowledge was imposed on my identity. For the defence of the interviewee, she might have acted otherwise if she had known my German background and the latter had insisted to like stories. However in that case deliberate confutation becomes a precondition for openness. In Levinasian ethics a decision to act re-sponsibly occurs prior to the interruption of the self. I do not intend to charge the interviewee of not being open, but rather point to the danger of knowledge that is treated like a fixed rule. If the individual does not take responsibility for her/his own actions and merely follows cultural norms of behaviour, (s)he risks to discard Levinasian openness and responsibility to the individual and the situation.

Levinasian ethics does not only serve as a basis for the deconstruction in this book, but also suggests ways how to avoid the limitations cultural knowledge entails. In this regard Levinas' idea to access signification without falling into the "trap" of any confining knowledge is discussed at this point. He saw significance emerge from an ethical event being the face-to face encounter (Levinas 2003). If the Other is given the opportunity to express a moral command, one can respond in a moral way. In order to reach the "essential and intelligible", access is only gained *through* culture, hence by direct and open exposure to it. In turn through access emerges significance. Hence the ethical encounter with the Other, which is not confined by pre-knowledge or prejudices, sets the stage for a "real" experience. If an ethical exposure is avoided or limited in its condition, "real" significance will be foreclosed. Cultural knowledge forecloses open exposure to the demand of the

Other due to its finality in providing cultural norms of behaviour. If the individual who adopts cultural knowledge takes the finality for granted and directs her/his behaviour according to the "information" gathered openness towards deviance is limited if not confined. As a consequence responsibility is shifted towards norms.

The Saying (re-sponsive communication) and the actual interaction and not the Said (pre-knowledge) gives room to a need of affection. Rhodes and Westwood ascribed more importance to affection than knowledge (Rhodes, Westwood 2007). Critchley understands the Saying as one's exposure to the Other, something that cannot be ascribed to any description (Critchley 1999). Hence Levinasian ethics focuses particularly on the actual interaction rather than on any "preparation" and therefore prejudgement occurring beforehand. "Preparation" in the Levinasian sense refers solely to the individual's deliberate decision to activate responsibility as well as let the Other interrupt the self. Moral imperatives are given more weight than symbolic forms and are therefore allowed to interrupt the latter (Levinas 2003).

Levinas stated this more explicitly:

> "The idea of a universal grammar and an algorithmic language built on the skeleton of that grammar must be abandoned. No direct or privileged contact with the world of Ideas is possible. Such a conception of universality translates the radical opposition […] against cultural expansion by colonization. Culture and colonization do not go together." ((Levinas 2003), p. 37)

He affirmed what was outlined by PCT: universal application of categories across cultures carries an aftertaste of colonization since Western discourse and understanding of reality is imposed on any culture on the globe. According to Levinas culture gains significance only through the moral transcendence of the Other. The central task should be to approach ambiguity in the right way. That is to say ethically, thus open and generous instead of avoiding or diminishing it. Further it is exactly in situations of uncertainty where ethics come to the fore since Levinas asks us to activate infinite responsibility and let the Other interrupt the self. And even if uncertainty and ambiguity do not experience any reduction a positive perspective on the issue can lead to new insights: Critchley and Bernasconi emphasized that "the end of certainty can be the beginning of trust" ((Critchley, Bernasconi 2002), p. 26).

To sum it up: since cultural knowledge is supposed to lead to certain ends, the individual who studies this knowledge is advised to adhere to it and let it direct the behaviour. The Levinasian perspective reveals however that knowledge forecloses openness to the individuality of the counterpart, the specificity of the situation and so on. It takes the responsibility from the individual who is also taken the freedom to gain real significance of the Other. Again cultural knowledge merely serves a purpose rather than the idea of tolerance and respect.

4.3.2.2 Constructing Knowledge as a Totality

This section is closely linked to previous arguments showing that cultural knowledge has been constituted from a Western point of view, meaning that the terms used reflect a Western understanding of reality (section 4.3.1.2). Further the arguments of homogenization and simplification are of relevance here as well. Levinas' concept of "totality" integrates these aspects. Aasland defines "totality" as a "closed, self-contained structure of meaning" ((Aasland 2007), p. 6). Or, as Peperzak et al. framed it in the preface of the book "Emmanuel Levinas: Basic Philosophical Writings":

> "Western thought and practice [in Levinas' view] are marked by a striving for totalization, in which the universe is reduced to an originary and ultimate unity by way of panoramic overviews and dialectical syntheses" (Levinas et al. 1996), p. X).

If individuals understand cultures in totalities they will reduce them "to an object in the mind of the self", meaning that the counterpart is first and foremost "translated" into one's own terms ((Aasland 2007), p. 4). Levinasian ethics however understands difference to be metaphysical and transcendent. Knowledge can therefore, even if multiple perspectives coin it never describe the Other and differences between individuals in a reliable way.

Levinasian ethics assertively dissents the perception that the more we know the better we will be able to understand. He understands the Other as "an undefined and immeasurable object of learning" that is impossible to dominate by imposed descriptions ((Ben-Ari, Strier 2010), p. 7). Difference to his mind is not ontological and visible, but rather transcendent and metaphysical (Muhr 2008a). Hence learning about the Other does not represent an adequate goal from a Levinasian perspective. He encourages each individual to build up a relation to difference. Even though a totality develops a certain relation to the Other it happens at the expense of a reduction in distance where opposition fades ((Rhodes, Westwood 2007), (Aasland 2007)). Totalities serve the goal of achieving certain ends.

However it all happens at the expense of foreclosed openness and responsibility towards otherness.

Is a totality therefore reflected in cultural knowledge? Here it makes sense to turn to the functionalist research paradigm Hall's, Hofstede's and Trompenaars' works account for. Functionalist approaches believe to resemble and represent reality in an accurate way. Validity and truthfulness are ascribed to research since the "mirroring" of reality is assumingly conducted in an accurate way. However in order to "mirror" reality in a functionalist sense, it needs to undergo simplification and fixation. Hence assuming that cultural knowledge can be abstracted by using rational research methods might be true in a functionalist sense. Fixation, limitation of reality and a simplified picture are the costly consequences of this assumption. As Jack and Westwood clearly stated:

> "science was interpellated as a superior knowledge system and provided the means for subjecting the Other to 'scientific' scrutiny in order to appropriate and represent knowledge about that Other" ((Jack, Westwood 2006), p. 491).

The goal to present knowledge about cultures justifies "scientific" scrutiny and the according conditions. It was stated earlier that cultural representations such as Hofstede's cultural dimensions are regarded to present a complete, neutral picture of reality. Thereby they account for a "closed, self-contained" piece of knowledge due to the epistemological and ontological limitations. Thus cultural representations represent a totality.

Illustrations in form of quotes from interviews and questionnaires were given in sections 4.3.1.2 and 4.3.1.3. The quotes showed how individuals used cultural knowledge to make sense of cultural differences by referring to a Western perception of reality. Further they illustrated how individuals tend to homogenize members of one nation with one culture. If those who acquired cultural knowledge are not aware of its construction as a totality, they, according to Levinas, miss nuances by ignoring the incomprehensibility of the Other. Accordingly, one will not be able to fully comprehend the Other and more importantly not be aware that cultural knowledge cannot account for everything.

I therefore found an answer in my search for respectful representations and interactions based on respect. Totalities simplify the Other and make members of other cultures "into the same". In this case, greater importance is ascribed to understanding (comprehension) than to a respectful representation. If individuals are not aware of these significant limitations, they are confined in their openness towards the Other as well as to the specificity of the situation. Levinasian ethics explores the limitations that cultural knowledge is exposed to. And these limitations are at the same time barriers towards tolerance, let alone respect.

4.3.2.3 Synthesis of the Levinasian Perspective

The two previous chapters explored the Levinasian perspective on cultural knowledge and exposed the limitations that act as significant barriers to respectful representations and interactions based on respect.

First it was outlined how knowledge has the power to replace individual responsibility that guides behaviour. In this regard it is considered final in the sense that openness to exceptions and deviance is foreclosed. As a consequence the student of cultural knowledge might miss the two latter points.

It was further described that abstracting knowledge by using rational research methods leads to a reduction of cultures into totalities, which reflect a limited picture of reality and prevent any openness to otherness. Opposition fades due to a process of reduction and "real" understanding is not achieved.

If cultural knowledge mainly aims to establish and maintain control, Levinasian ethics constitutes a significant challenge of the same. It does not leave room for any intention of control. A Levinasian perspective revealed two of the downsides of aiming at control in the intercultural encounter. The intention here is not to instruct cultural knowledge, but to point at limitations that have been accepted for the sake of control. Consequences for those who adopt cultural knowledge from a Levinasian perspective are the following: a real, open encounter and a relation to difference is hindered if cultural knowledge is meticulously followed. Furthermore, application of cultural knowledge without being aware of its limitations would jeopardize humanity, tolerance and respect.

5   Conclusion and Future Outlook

5.1   CONCLUSIONS OF THIS BOOK

With this book cultural knowledge was deconstructed in order to open it up to new perspectives. The concept presents itself as the foundation for understanding as well as respect for cultural differences. The interviews and literature cited have stressed the importance of respect that welcomes support in this regard (see in particular 4.2). This book underscored the importance of the same and took a critical perspective on cultural knowledge. It analyzed how cultural knowledge accounts for respectful representations and to what extent the discourse contributes to respect for cultural differences.

With these issues in mind ethical deconstruction was employed to discuss the RQ:

> How does cultural knowledge represent cultures and how may this prevent rather than encourage interactions based on respect for cultural differences?

The starting points for the analysis were laid out by PCT and Levinasian ethics. Some of their main arguments presented the potential limitations of cultural knowledge. After demonstrating one argument, its reflection in cultural knowledge was analyzed. The results of the interviews and questionnaires illustrated how the limitation of cultural knowledge is translated into practice. This was followed by a discussion on the consequences for those who acquire cultural knowledge and are not aware of its limitations.

The limitations outlined referred to the constitution of cultural differences as a threat, which leads to a negative perception of the same. The same consequence occurred in terms of the second limitation. It pointed at the illustration of cultural differences in binary oppositions from a Western perspective. If students are not aware of the one-sidedness of binary oppositions, they tend to see differences in extremes where one end is good and the other end is bad. The PCT-perspective further revealed homogenization and simplification of cultures and the relevant factors respectively. Those who adopt cultural knowledge are limited in their understanding of cultural differences and therefore hampered in their openness to the individuality of the counterpart and the specificity of the intercultural situation.

Levinasian ethics indicated how responsibility is shifted from the individual towards knowledge. Further it revealed how knowledge is framed in totalities. Both of the sections led to the conclusion that freedom is taken from individuals who acquire cultural knowledge to openly and responsibly interact with the Other. This occurs if they adhere to (totalised) knowledge without paying attention to any exceptions and context.

At the beginning of this book it was claimed that respectful representations of cultures are an important condition for respect towards cultural differences. The analysis revealed that cultural knowledge shows constraints in that regard since others are culturally portrayed in a one-sided, biased and simplified way. Thus the limitations lead to significant consequences and limits that can undermine respect for cultural differences. The main concern was centred on the subjugation of an open and respectful encounter to the goal of control. Aspects such as trust, respect and honesty are diverted if control cannot be accounted for.

Based on the analysis, I conclude that interests of control have primarily influenced the constitution of cultural knowledge. The business context expects cultural knowledge to serve as a tool that promotes successful transaction in business. As a consequence of this fundamental condition, cultural knowledge has shifted its priorities. The ultimate goal of control and successful business transactions ranks first. Cultural knowledge has undergone certain modulations in order to represent a valuable tool and to serve the ultimate end. Respect for cultural differences is sustained as long as it does not interfere with interests of control. In this sense, understanding and respect are not treated on equal terms. Thus what cultural knowledge "promises" is not kept in the end since the claim to developed understanding *and* respect is not fulfilled. First of all "understanding" is compromised due to one-sidedness, homogenization and so forth and therefore limited in its *respectful* representation. Thus it is questionable as a "real" and reliable source in the comprehension of cultural differences. Secondly it hampers respect towards cultural differences particularly in terms of openness and positive attitude.

In response to the RQ this book therefore concludes that the task to create cultural knowledge for the sake of control was more powerful than the idea of an ethical/justified representation of the Other. The consequential limitations lead in turn to consequences that impair intercultural encounters based on respect for cultural differences. Therefore cultural knowledge shows substantial constraints in that regard. Goal-oriented knowledge and the respective conditions have been privileged to the guiding idea of respect for cultural differences.

This book aimed to make room for a point of otherness, namely true respect for cultural differences in and through cultural knowledge. The study pointed to the limits that Western authorship may have imposed. In so doing, blind spots within cultural knowledge that challenge the stability of its dominant interpretation were revealed. Thus the study hopes to have made a contribution to opening up cultural knowledge for improvement and/or alternatives. And more importantly, I exerted my best effort in creating an awareness of limitations and according consequences that are particularly important for those who acquire the knowledge. However, it also occurred that students/participants of ICT who learned about cultural knowledge were not aware of its limitations. This book therefore shall also present a plea for trainers or teachers of ICT to become acquainted with the limitations of cultural knowledge and transfer this knowledge to their students.

5.2 LIMITATIONS

Limitations with respect to the data have already been discussed in section 2.4. This section deals with the limitations concerning the theory and method used. The theory consisted of PCT and Levinasian ethics. PCT is limited due to its Eurocentric focus. Even though PCT criticized Western dominance when it came to representations of colonized countries, its treatment of cultural knowledge was largely done from a Western perspective. The same applies for Levinasian ethics. It also accounts for me, the author of this book, since I was influenced by my European background which affected the style of writing and the words used. One of the main criticisms raised in this book is one-sidedness. However, it did not give a voice to the objects of cultural knowledge either. And last but not least cultural knowledge was judged on the grounds of freedom and liberty, particularly when it came to tolerance for cultural difference. Thus western values served as the foundation of this book.

Ethical deconstruction was employed as a method in this book. Methodological concerns have already been stated. It was argued that alterity is demised as soon as the results of deconstruction are put into words. Herewith the (similar) dilemma of framing deconstruction in any kind of definition or process shall be outlined. Critchley claims that any ontological statement of deconstruction represents a contradiction to the idea of the former (Critchley 1999). Even Derrida himself avoided to define deconstruction. Beardsworth explains Derrida's concern by stating that alterity is (once more) given up as soon as deconstruction is described and procedural steps are advised (Beardsworth 1996). The critical reader adheres to the steps a method entails and therefore restricts her-

/himself in the actual process of (critical/clotural) reading. Furthermore deconstruction turns into a prejudicial procedure where the reader has already a judgement in mind that (s)he aims to reveal in a text. The same occurred in this book to a certain extent: due to my first introduction to Levinas I kept wondering whether cultural knowledge constitutes a reliable foundation for respect for cultural differences. A sceptical attitude was therefore given right from the start. However the book tried to counter the outlined dilemma by looking at various forms of data in order to underpin the arguments made.

5.3   FUTURE RESEARCH

This book was mainly interested in a critical (clotural) reading of cultural knowledge. However it did not aim to give solutions to the particular limitations outlined. Even though the book introduced the approaches of Bhabha, Spivak and ultimately Levinas who dealt with some of the limitations, I am aware that translating their theories into practice remains a challenge. The book therefore serves as a starting point for future research, particularly regarding pragmatic suggestions to solve the problems posed by the limitations outlined in the study and the possible consequences that these limitations might lead to.

The book especially paid attention to the aspect of awareness. I believe that many of the consequences discussed are a result of the student's lack of awareness of the limitations inherent in cultural knowledge. Hence future research could investigate how the awareness of limitations changes peoples' perception of cultural knowledge and their attitude towards other cultures. Further future research could look into how awareness cannot only affect knowledge and attitude but more importantly, how this awareness can lead to a change in behaviour towards the Other in a way that is ethical.

In addition, I envision future research as giving voice to the subjects of cultural knowledge. In chapter 3 it was stated that PCT-scholars suggested including the voice of the Other in cultural representation. In this respect, I propose the inclusion of the voice of the Other in order to reflect on the consequences outlined. If the "victims" of these consequences were given room to express themselves then the extent to which they feel respected in their cultural circumstances through cultural knowledge as constituted by Hall, Hofstede and Trompenaars would be disclosed.

References

Aasland, D.G. 2007, "The Exteriority Of Ethics In Management And Its Transition Into Justice: A Levinasian Approach To Ethics In Business", *Business Ethics: A European Review,* vol. 16, no. 3, pp. 220-226.

Aasland, D.G. 2004, "On The Ethics Behind "Business Ethics"", *Journal of Business Ethics,* vol. 53, no. 2, pp. 3-8.

Adorno, T.W., Horkheimer, M. & Cumming, J. 1979, *Dialectic Of Enlightenment,* Verso Editions : [Distributed by NLB], London.

Alvesson, M. 2003, "Beyond Neopositivists, Romantics And Localists: A Reflexive Approach To Interviews In Organizational Research", *The Academy of Management Review,* vol. 28, no. 1, pp. 13-33.

Alvesson, M. & Deetz, S.A. 1999, *Doing Critical Management Research,* Sage, Thousand Oaks, Calif.

Ashcroft, B., Griffiths, G. & Tiffin, H. 1998, *Key Concepts in Post-Colonial Studies,* Routledge, London; New York.

Bauman, Z. 2004, *Postmodern Ethics,* Blackwell, Oxford.

Beardsworth, R. 1996, *Derrida & the political,* Routledge, London; New York.

Ben-Ari, A. & Strier, R. 2010, "Rethinking Cultural Competence: What Can We Learn From Levinas?", vol. 1, pp. 1-13.

Bevan, D. & Corvellec, H. 2007, "The Impossibility Of Corporate Ethics: For A Levinasian Approach To Managerial Ethics", *Business Ethics: A European Review,* vol. 16, no. 3, pp. 208-219.

Bhabha, H.K. 1994, *The Location Of Culture,* Routledge, London; New York.

Bjerregaard, T., Lauring, J. & Klitmøller, A. 2009, "A Critical Analysis Of Intercultural Communication Research In Cross-Cultural Management: Introducing Newer Developments In Anthropology", *Critical Perspectives On International Business,* vol. 5, no. 3, pp. 207-228.

Black, J.S. & Mendenhall, M. 1990, "Cross-Cultural Training Effectiveness: A Review and a Theoretical Framework for Future Research", *Academy of Management Review,* vol. 15, no. 1, pp. 113-136.

Blasco, M. 2004, "Stranger To Us Than The Birds In Our Garden?" in *Intercultural Alternatives,* eds. M. Blasco & J. Gustafsson, Business School Press, Copenhagen, pp. 19-41.

Brislin, R.W. & Yoshida, T. 1994, *Intercultural Communication: Introduction,* Sage Pubns.

Calás, M.B. & Smircich, L. 1999, "Past Postmodernism? Reflections And Tentative Directions", *Academy of Management Review,* vol. 24, no. 4, pp. 649-671.

Caligiuri, P., Phillips, J., Lazarova, M., Tarique, I. & Burgi, P. 2001, "The Theory Of Met Expectations Applied To Expatriate Adjustment: The Role Of Crosscultural Training", *International Journal of Human Resource Management,* vol. 12, no. 3, pp. 357-372.

Caligiuri, P.M. 2000, "Selecting Expatriates For Personality Characteristics: A Moderating Effect Of Personality On The Relationship Between Host National Contact And Cross-cultural Adjustment", *Management International Review,* vol. 40, pp. 61-80.

Cooper, R. 1992, *Formal Organization As Representation: Remote Control, Displacement And Abbreviation,* Sage Publications, London; New York.

Critchley, S. 1999, *The Ethics Of Deconstruction; Derrida And Levinas,* 2nd edn, Edinburgh University Press, Edinburgh.

Critchley, S. & Bernasconi, R. 2002, *The Cambridge Companion To Levinas,* Cambridge University Press, Cambridge.

Day, K.D. 1998, "Fostering Respect For Other Cultures In Teaching Intercultural Communication" in *Civic Discourse: Multiculturalism, Cultural Diversity and Global*

Communication, eds. K.S. Sitaram & M.H. Prosser, Ablex Pub. Corp., Stamford, Conn., pp. 133.

Derrida, J., Habermas, J. & Thomassen, L. 2006, *The Derrida-Habermas Reader,* Edinburgh University Press, Edinburgh.

Dumont, J.-. & Lemaître, G. 2005, *Counting Immigrants And Expatriates In OECD Countries: A New Perspective,* OECD, Paris.

Earley, P.C. 1987, "Intercultural Training For Managers: A Comparison Of Documentary And Interpersonal Methods", *Academy of Management Journal,* vol. 30, no. 4, pp. 685-698.

Easterby-Smith, M., Thorpe, R. & Jackson, P. 2008, *Management Research,* 3rd edn, Sage, London.

Encyclopaedia Britannica 2010, , *Structural Functionalism.* Available: http://www.britannica.com/EBchecked/topic/504562/rite-of-passage/283997/Structural-functionalism?anchor=ref1053266 [2010, 08/22] .

Engelbert, S. 2004, "'Intercultural Training' In Exchange Situations For Experts And Management: A Critical Reflection", *Intercultural Education,* vol. 15, no. 2, pp. 195-208.

Fougere, M. & Moulettes, A. 2007, "The Construction Of The Modern West And The Backward Rest: Studying the Discourse of Hofstede's Culture's Consequences", *Journal of Multicultural Discourse,* vol. 2, no. 1, pp. 1-19.

Gudykunst, W.B. 1995, "Anxiety / Uncertainty Management (AUM) Theory" in *Intercultural Communication Theory,* ed. R. Wiseman, Sage, London, pp. 8-58.

Gudykunst, W.B. & Mody, B. 2002, *Handbook Of International And Intercultural Communication,* 2nd edn, Sage Publications, London.

Hall, E.T. 1976, *Beyond Culture,* Anchor Books: Doubleday, New York, NY.

Hall, E.T. 1966, *The Hidden Dimension,* Doubleday, Garden City, N.Y.

Hall, E.T. 1959, *The Silent Language,* Doubleday, Garden City, N.Y.

Hall, E.T. 1955, *The Anthropology Of Manners,* W.H. Freeman, San Francisco.

Hammer, M.R. 2000, "Intercultural Communication Competence" in *Handbook Of International And Intercultural Communication,* eds. M.K. Asante, W.B. Gudykunst & E. Newmark, Sage, Newbury Park, pp. 247-258.

Hickling-Hudson, A. 2003, "Multicultural Education And The Postcolonial Turn", *Policy Futures in Education,* vol. 1, no. 2, pp. 381-401.

Hofstede, G.H. 1991, *Cultures And Organizations: Software Of The Mind,* McGraw-Hill, London; New York.

Hofstede, G.H. 1980, *Culture's Consequences : International Differences In Work-related Values,* Sage Publications, Beverly Hills, Calif.

itim Culture and Management Consultancy 2009, , *Geert Hofstede Cultural Dimensions.* Available: http://www.geert-hofstede.com/ [2010, 09/05] .

Jack, G. & Lorbiecki, A. 2003, "Asserting Possibilities Of Resistance In The Cross-Cutural Teaching Machine: Re-viewing Videos Of Others" in *Postcolonial Theory And Organizational Analysis: A Critical Engagement,* ed. A. Prasad, Palgrave Macmillan, New York, pp. 213-234.

Jack, G. & Westwood, R. 2006, "Postcolonialism And The Politics Of Qualitative Research In International Business", *Management International Review,* vol. 46, no. 4, pp. 481-501.

Jaeger, K. 1995, "Teaching Culture - State Of The Art" in *Intercultural Competence: A new Challenge for Language Teachers and Trainers in Europe,* eds. A.A. Jensen, K. Jaeger & A. Lorentsen, Centre for Languages and Intercultural Studies, Denmark, pp. 31-52.

Jeanes, E. & Muhr, S.L. 2010, "The Impossibility Of Guidance – A Levinasian Critique Of Business Ethics" in *Ethics And Organizational Practice – Questioning The Moral Foundations Of Management,* eds. S.L. Muhr, B.M. Sorensen & S. Vallentin, Edward Elgar Publishing Limited, Cheltenham, pp. 143-162.

Johnson, B. 1981, *The Critical Difference : Essays In The Contemporary Rhetoric Of Reading,* Johns Hopkins University Press, Baltimore.

Kapoor, I. 2004, "Hyper-Self-Reflexive Development? Spivak On Representing The Third World 'Other'", *Third World Quarterly,* vol. 25, no. 4, pp. 627-647.

Kelemen, M. & Rumens, N. 2008, *An Introduction To Critical Management Research,* Sage Publications, Los Angeles, CA.

Kim, D., Pan, Y. & Park, H.S. 1998, "High- Versus Low-Context Culture: A Comparison Of Chinese, Korean, And American Cultures", *Psychology & Marketing,* vol. 15, no. 6, pp. 507-521.

Kim, M.-. 2007, "Our Culture, Their Culture And Beyond: Further Thoughts On Ethnocentrism In Hofstede's Discourse", *Journal of Multicultural Discourse,* vol. 2, no. 1, pp. 26-31.

Klein, A.C. 1995, *Meeting The Great Bliss Queen: Buddhists, Feminists And The Art Of The Self,* Beacon Press, Boston.

Kwek, D. 2003, "Decolonizing and Re-Presenting Culture's Consequences: A Postcolonial Critique of Cross-Cultural Studies in Manangement" in *Postcolonial Theory and Organisational Analysis: A Critical Engagemen*t, ed. A. Prasad, Palgrave Macmillan, Basingstoke, pp. 121-146.

Leiba-O'Sullivan, S. 1999, "The Distinction Between Stable And Dynamic Cross-cultural Competencies: Implications For Expatriate Trainability", *Journal of International Business Studies,* vol. 30, no. 4, pp. 709-725.

Levinas, E. 2003, *Humanism Of The Other,* University of Illinois Press, Urbana; Chicago.

Levinas, E. 1981, *Otherwise Than Being: Or, Beyond Essence,* M. Nijhoff ; Distributors for the U.S. and Canada, Kluwer Boston, Hague; Boston; Hingham, MA.

Levinas, E. 1969, *Totality And Infinity; An Essay On Exteriority,* Duquesne University Press, Pittsburgh.

Levinas, E., Peperzak, A.T., Critchley, S. & Bernasconi, R. 1996, *Emmanuel Levinas: Basic Philosophical Writings,* Indiana University Press, Bloomington.

Loacker, B. & Muhr, S.L. 2009, "How Can I Become A Responsible Subject? Towards A Practice-Based Ethics Of Responsiveness", *Journal of Business Ethics,* vol. 90, no. 2, pp. 265-277.

Loosemore, M. & Lee, P. 2002, "Communication Problems With Ethnic Minorities In The Construction Industry", *International journal of project management : the journal of the International Project Management Association.,* vol. 20, no. 7, pp. 517-524.

Mc Leod, J. 2000, *Beginning Postcolonialism,* Manchester University Press : St. Martin's Press, Manchester; New York.

Mishra, V. & Hodge, B. 1994, "What is Post(-)colonialism?" in *Colonial Discourse And Post-Colonial Theory: A Reade*r, eds. P. Williams & L. Chrisman, Columbia University Press, New York, pp. 276-290.

Morris, M.A. & Robie, C. 2001, "A Meta-analysis Of The Effects Of Cross-cultural Training On Expatriate Performance And Adjustment", *International Journal of Training and Development,* vol. 5, no. 2, pp. 112-125.

Muhr, S.L. 2008a, "Othering Diversity - A Levinasian Analysis Of Diversity Management", *International Journal Of Management Concepts and Philosophy,* vol. 3, no. 2, pp. 176-189.

Muhr, S.L. 2008b, "Reflections On Responsibility And Justice, Coaching Human Rights In South Africa", *Management Decision,* vol. 46, no. 8, pp. 1175-1186.

Munshi, D. & McKie, D. 2001, "Toward A New Cartography Of Intercultural Communication: Mapping Blas, Business, And Diversity", *Business communication quarterly : a publication of the Association for Business Communication.,* vol. 64, no. 3, pp. 9.

Noerregard, J.L. 2004, "Intercultural Ethics: A Hermeneutic Approach To Ethics In Intercultural Communication " in *Intercultural Alternatives*, eds. M. Blasco & J. Gustafsson, Business School Press, Copenhagen, pp. 193-213.

Onkvisit, S. & Shaw, J.J. 1993, *International Marketing: Analysis And Strategy,* Macmillan Pub. Co., New York.

Pieper, A. 2009, *Introduction To Philosophical Ethics (transl. by author)* , Fernuniversitaet Hagen, Hagen, Germany.

Prasad, A. 2003, *Postcolonial Theory And Organizational Analysis: A Critical Engagement,* Palgrave Macmillan, Basingstoke.

Princeton University 2010, *, Lexical Database for English.* Available: http://wordnetweb.princeton.edu/perl/webwn?s=deconstruction [2010, 2001, 07/25].

Pusch, M.D. 2004, "Intercultural Training In Historical Perspective" in *Handbook of Intercultural Training,* eds. D. Landis, J.M. Bennett & M.J. Bennett, 3rd edn, Sage Publications, London, pp. 13-36.

Rhodes, C. & Westwood, R. 2007, "Letting Knowledge Go: Ethics and Representation of the Other in International and Cross-Cultural Management " in , ed. C. Carter, Edward Elgar, Cheltenham, pp. 57-72.

Rogers, E.M., Hart, W.B. & Miike, Y. 2002, "Edward T. Hall And The History Of Intercultural Communication: The United States And Japan", *Keio Communication Review,* vol. 24, pp. 3-26.

Rosenthal, S.B. 2003, "A Time For Being Ethical: Levinas And Pragmatism", *Journal of Speculative Philosophy,* vol. 17, no. 3, pp. 192-203.

Sackmann, S. & Phillips, M. 2004, "Contextual Influences on Culture Research", *International Journal of Cross Cultural Management,* vol. 4, no. 3, pp. 370-390.

Said, E.W. 1978, *Orientalism,* Routledge and Kegan Paul.

Saunders, M., Lewis, P. & Thornhill, A. 2007, *Research Methods for Business Students,* Financial Times Prentice Hall, Harlow [u.a.].

Scott, A. no year, *, Review Of Emmanuel Levinas's "Totality And Infinity".* Available: http://www.angelfire.com/md2/timewarp/levinas.html [2010, 08/22] .

Shaffer, M.A., Harrison, D.A., Gregersen, H., Black, J.S. & Ferzandi, L.A. 2006, "You Can Take It With You: Individual Differences And Expatriate Effectiveness", *Journal of Applied Psychology,* vol. 91, no. 1, pp. 109-125.

Soderberg, A.-. & Holden, N. 2002, "Rethinking Cross-cultural Management In a Globalizing Business World", *Communication Abstracts,* vol. 25, no. 6, pp. 755-909.

Soendergaard, M. 1994, "Research Note: Hofstede's Consequences: A Study of Reviews, Citations and Replications", *Organization Studies,* vol. 15, no. 3, pp. 447-456.

Spivak, G.C. 1993a, *Outside In The Teaching Machine,* Routledge, New York.

Spivak, G.C. 1993b, "The Politics Of Translation" in *Outside In The Teaching Machine,* ed. G.C. Spivak, Routledge, New York, pp. 179-200.

Spivak, G.C. 1990, "The Post-Modern Condition: The End Of Politics?" in *The Post-Colonial Critic: Interviews, Strategies And Dialogues,* eds. G.C. Spivak & S. Harasym, Routledge, New York, pp. 17-34.

Spivak, G.C. 1988, *Can The Subaltern Speak?* Macmillan, Basingstoke.

Szkudlarek, B. 2009, "Through Western Eyes: Insights Into The Intercultural Training Field", *Organization Studies,* vol. 30, no. 9, pp. 975-986.

Trompenaars, F. 1993, *Riding The Waves Of Culture: Understanding Cultural Diversity In Business,* Economist Books, London.

Tung, R.L. 1987, "Expatriate Assignments: Enhancing Success and Minimizing Failure", *The Academy of Management Executive,* vol. 1, no. 2, pp. 117-125.

Vaara, E., Tienari, J., Piekkari, R. & Säntti, R. 2005, "Language And The Circuits Of Power In a Merging Multinational Corporation", *Journal of Management Studies,* vol. 42, no. 3, pp. 595-623.

Voce, A. 2004, *, Introduction To Research Paradigms.* Available: http://familymedicine.ukzn.ac.za/Uploads/131e81cf-f876-4e8d-9016-69ec7d6598b8/Introduction%20to%20research%20paradigms.doc [2010, 08/14] .

Walle, A.H. 1990, "Beyond The Ugly American", *Management Decision,* vol. 28, no. 7, pp. 11-16.

Westwood, R. 2006, "International Business And Management Studies As An Orientalist Discourse: A Postcolonial Critique", *Critical Perspectives on International Business,* vol. 2, no. 2, pp. 91-113.

Westwood, R. & Jack, G. 2007, "Manifesto for a post-colonial international business and management studies ", vol. 3, no. 3, pp. 246-265.

Xue, D. 2003, *Development Of A Culture-adequate Concept For Intercultural Training: Example: Intercultural Training for Chinese As Preparation For Business Cooperation With Germans (transl. by author).*

Young, R. 2000, *Post-Colonialism: An Historical Introduction,* Blackwell.

.

CPSIA information can be obtained
at www.ICGtesting.com
Printed in the USA
LVHW061513170123
737251LV00012B/1221

9 783842 862630